MW01051327

Whole Grain
SOURDOUGH
at Home

Whole Grain SOURDOUGH at Home

The Simple Way to Bake Artisan Bread with Whole Wheat, Einkorn, Spelt, Rye and Other Ancient Grains

Elaine Boddy

Founder of foodbod Sourdough

PAGE STREET
PUBLISHING CO.

PAGE STREET
PUBLISHING CO.

Copyright © 2020 Elaine Boddy

First published in 2020 by
Page Street Publishing Co.
27 Congress Street, Suite 105
Salem, MA 01970
www.pagestreetpublishing.com

All rights reserved. No part of this book may be reproduced or used, in any form or by any means, electronic or mechanical, without prior permission in writing from the publisher.

Distributed by Macmillan, sales in Canada by The Canadian Manda Group.

24   23   22   21   3   4   5   6

ISBN-13: 978-1-64567-110-7
ISBN-10: 1-64567-110-0

Library of Congress Control Number: 2019957258

Cover and book design by Molly Gillespie for Page Street Publishing Co.
Photography by James Kennedy

Printed and bound in the United States

Page Street Publishing protects our planet by donating to nonprofits like The Trustees, which focuses on local land conservation.

For Caroline and Selma,
never forgotten xx

Contents

Introduction

Welcome to my wonderful world of sourdough.

I love sourdough. I love every aspect of making it, from start to finish, or should I say from "starter" to finish? The whole process makes my heart sing, and you get great bread at the end of it—it is a win-win!

Sourdough is the oldest and most natural form of making leavened, or risen, bread and also the healthiest form of bread. It tastes wonderful and is fun to make. It is also so much simpler to make than you may think; the making and nurturing of the dough and baking of your own loaves can very easily and quickly become your homemade household staple.

I am a self-taught home baker; I bake bread for my family, in a standard domestic oven, in a typical home kitchen, with everyday ingredients that are easily accessible and with kitchen equipment that is readily available and inexpensive. That is what this book will enable you to do, too. Here you will find methods that I have used in my home kitchen every week for many years and have perfected with every baked and sourdough creation I have produced.

I have been told that I break all the "rules" when it comes to creating sourdough; but as far as I am concerned, there are no rules. Sourdough is not defined by looks, by a process or by certain handling, but by being made with a wild yeast starter. It should be simple, accessible and achievable for anyone who wants to give it a try. I have created a process that is done entirely in the bowl—no heavy kneading involved. There is also no need to turn out the dough onto a counter, no need for flour all over your kitchen, no need for any mess at all. It has been called a one-bowl wonder.

In this book, you will not find ratios, percentages or scientific explanations nor long-winded recipes, overcomplicated processes or unnecessary steps. You will not find trendy terminology, acronyms, excessive methodology or anything that may seem off-putting or scary.

What you will find are straightforward, simple steps, a wealth of hints and tips and a smooth path to sourdough success using a whole range of flours, in particular whole grains and ancient grains.

Sourdough is a wonderful way to create beautiful bread in so many ways—the possibilities are endless!

I am very excited to share my sourdough world with you and I hope that you enjoy this book as much as the bread you will be able to create.

Here's to baking great homemade sourdough. Happy baking!

Elaine
x   x

Whole Grain Sourdough Success

FLOUR

Sourdough is a simple thing; it truly is far easier to make than you may think. All it requires is a healthy, happy starter plus good flour, good water, a bit of salt, gentle handling, patience and understanding. Learn how to use your starter and you are already on the right track. Match that with good flour to build up a good structure in the dough, and success will be yours.

I cannot emphasize enough how important your choice of flour is to making sourdough. The fact is, not all flours are equal, and therefore they do not all do the same job.

In bygone times, there would have been far fewer options, but with progress and advancement, we now have an endless range of flours available to us all over the world. So, the challenge is to find what works best for you and your sourdough in your country. The key is a good, strong flour, especially if you are new to sourdough.

"Strong" Flour

The long proofing time required to create sourdough, especially whole grain sourdough, is best supported by using at least some "strong" flour, also commonly called bread flour, in the mixture. This helps the dough keep its integrity and structure during and after all that work it will do, plus it gives the dough an elasticity and allows it to be stretched without breaking when the pulls and folds are performed to build up the structure of the dough. Whole grain and ancient-grain flours add different flavors and textures to dough, but they all perform differently; these flours therefore require extra considerations. For example, some ancient-grain flours are weaker than our modern bread flours and work best with slightly less water and partnered with a stronger flour, whereas whole wheat flour benefits from a slightly longer initial rest to make it more supple to work with. These characteristics have all been accounted for in my recipes, to make it as simple as possible to use these flours in your bakes.

"Strong" flour tends to be milled from hard wheats. It is often called strong bread flour, which refers to the protein strength of the flour that comes from the gluten in the flour. The strong white bread flour I use has about 12.7 percent protein. Sourdough is termed a "free-form" bread—as typically it is not baked in a loaf pan, it lacks the support of the pan to hold the dough and give it shape; consequently, the dough needs to be strong enough to hold its own form while it bakes.

Some flours are sold with their protein percentage printed on the bag, but sadly, most do not. The protein percentage differs slightly from the nutritional protein stated on the bag, but the nutritional values table is a useful guide. For example, the bag of the strong white bread flour that I use lists that it contains 13.3 grams of nutritional protein per 100 grams of flour, which would make it 13.3 percent protein. The actual protein content of the gluten in the flour for our purposes is 12.7 percent.

In comparison, flours typically used for making other baked goods are weaker, milled from soft wheat, and contain only 9 to 10 percent protein.

Whole Grain Flours

Whether you call a flour whole meal, whole wheat or whole grain, such a flour includes, as the name suggests, the entire grain, as opposed to flours that have had the bran and wheat germ removed. Whole grain flours are packed with nutrients and flavor. They produce beautiful breads, often denser than loaves made with refined white flours.

Whole wheat flours tend to be stronger than white flours. While they take longer to soak up water, in the end whole wheat flours will typically absorb more water than white flour will, so these loaves typically benefit from being made with more water.

I often use whole wheat flour in recipes that additionally contain lighter flours, but I have also included a 100% whole wheat loaf (page 54).

Ancient-Grain Flours

I am a huge fan of grains—many of my meals are grain based—so to include them in my loaves is a joy for me. They add texture, flavor and wholesomeness, as well as history and a link back to a wonderful past of bread making. Ancient grains offer a new experience when adding them to dough and always enhance a loaf.

Our oldest grains, from which the first breads were made, have gained renewed popularity and are being widely used again. They are wonderfully tasty as whole grains, as well as flours, and add great flavors and textures to your bread, in addition to extra nutrients.

Special considerations and allowances may be necessary when ancient-grain flours are used to make sourdough, as they behave differently than our newer flours. They benefit from being supported by strong flour or used with other flours that complement them. These flours can be challenging, especially to a new baker, if used on their own, so I have provided tips and details to ensure your baking success.

Einkorn

Einkorn is the oldest of the ancient grains; this flavorful whole grain flour is fine with a yellow tint. It cannot hold its structure if used in a loaf on its own—as it proofs and grows, it becomes spongy and cannot be pulled and stretched—so it needs to be used differently. It is perfect when used along with another flour in a dough, though even then, you will still feel a stickiness in the dough.

Having said all that, I love it! It is possibly my favorite of the ancient grains.

In the United Kingdom, we have access to only whole grain einkorn, which is the kind I use in most of my recipes. In the United States, however, einkorn is available as an all-purpose flour that is lighter and has a different consistency and outcome.

Emmer

Emmer is also considered one of the earliest grains used to make bread. It is slightly nutty and wonderfully wholesome, whether used as a flour or whole grain. Emmer flour tends to be whole grain and is a fine but slightly grainy flour compared to einkorn. Although it absorbs water quickly and can make your dough sticky, its flavor and additional nutritional value make it worth working with.

Khorasan

Khorasan grain flour, also called kamut, is typically a whole grain flour, so it is stronger than other ancient-grain flours, but still it is ideally complemented with another flour in a dough as, used on its own, it will generate a very dense loaf. Khorasan flour is grainier than the other ancient-grain flours, and might initially make the dough feel stiffer, but it will then give and soften as you work with the dough, as well as impart a lovely nuttiness to the finished loaf.

Rye

Rye flour is milled from whole rye berries or the grain from rye grass. It is available as a whole grain or light flour, depending on how it has been milled.

Rye can be sticky and challenging to work with, but adds nutritional value as well as great depth of flavor to any bread. I typically use only a small amount of it in a dough rather than making high-percentage rye doughs.

Spelt

Spelt flour is ground from an ancient grain that was discovered after the previously discussed grains. As a flour, although it is not gluten-free, it is very kind on the digestive system and can be tolerated by many people who have dietary issues.

White spelt flour is very soft and fine. It is not strong enough to be used to make a loaf that can stand on its own unless you bake the dough in a pan to provide structure. Whole grain spelt is a bit stronger as it has the benefit of not having the bran sifted out, but it will still need some support.

I often use white spelt flour as an alternative to all-purpose flour in cakes and other baked goods, as well as to even out the density of heavier flours in my loaves. It is a very useful and versatile flour to have in the cupboard.

Note: Einkorn, emmer and spelt grains often can be found under the name "farro."

Throughout the book, I offer notes and tips about using these flours successfully to make starters as well as to make and bake my sourdoughs.

Around the world, the flours of a country have varying protein contents based on the breads that are typically baked there, and you will benefit from doing a bit of research into the flours that are available to you.

I would always advise experimenting with different flours once you have come to grips with sourdoughs and their starters, but when you first come to sourdough, make your life easy by keeping it simple and consistent. Your starter is the key to everything and it needs to be strong, healthy and active to work well for you, so give it the best possible flour you can, and stick with it. If it is happy and responsive and loving life, do not change anything about it.

By sourcing great flour, you give yourself the best chance for sourdough success.

Flour and Water

Different flours, let alone the same flours from different countries, absorb water differently. Some strong flours I have used have absorbed more water than others, making the dough stickier and looser to handle, which new sourdough bakers may find off-putting. If this is the case for you, try using a little less water in the recipe you are following. Getting to know the flour that is available to you and how to use it will help your sourdough journey.

INGREDIENTS AND EQUIPMENT

The following is a list of what you ideally need to make a starter and my master recipe; these are my recommendations and are the items that I always use. You can purchase substitutions for some of these items, or you may easily find alternatives in your own kitchen. It might seem like a lot to assemble initially, but if you use them week after week, you will see that it is worth the investment. For example, I have used the same pans to bake my loaves right from the beginning and they are still working perfectly and look like new.

These are the things I would definitely recommend that you have:

Good-quality flour: See page 11.

Water: Water can be as crucial to the success of your sourdough as the flour you use.

Your tap water may well be safe enough to use, but initially I always suggest using filtered water, or boiled and cooled tap water, until you are familiar with the sourdough process.

If your tap water is heavily chlorinated, filling a jug with it and leaving it to stand for 24 hours will cause the chlorine to evaporate. If your tap water is not of good quality for other reasons, it could kill your starter and ruin your dough. Once your starter is established, test a small portion by feeding it with flour and your tap water and see how it responds, but never risk your whole starter until you know the water will not adversely affect it.

Small glass bowl or jar with a fitted lid: This is for making and storing your starter. I use glass bowls that are 6¾ inches (17 cm) in diameter with fitted lids. I prefer glass to plastic, as glass does not absorb flavors or aromas from other foods; and glass rather than ceramic, as it is a joy to see the activity in the starter down the sides and bottom of the mixture. This size bowl also works to prevent you from keeping too much starter.

Large mixing bowl: I like using glass bowls as they allow you to see the wonderful texture of your dough and the dough does not stick to the bowl too much, but any kind of large ceramic bowl will work, too. The glass mixing bowls that I use are 9 inches (23 cm) in diameter and 3½ inches (9 cm) deep. Their size also helps me assess the growth of the dough, which you may also find useful.

Digital scale: A scale really is necessary. It makes a big difference to baking to be able to weigh all the ingredients, but especially when making and maintaining a starter. Inexpensive scales are easy to find and work fine for the purposes of sourdough baking as long as you are sure of their accuracy. Use the tare function on your scale to reset the weight in between each ingredient addition. It is even easier than using measuring cups! In case you do not have access to a scale, I have provided U.S. volume measurements for the recipes in this book.

A room thermometer: Sourdough is so affected by temperature that a thermometer is a very useful item to have in your kitchen. It will help plan and nurture your doughs, coax them through cold temperatures and protect them during high temperatures.

Shower caps or tea towels: Clean shower caps are the perfect creative tool to use for covering bowls of dough and bannetons during the proofing time. After each use, hang them, inside out, around the kitchen to dry, then shake off any dried dough and store them to use again and again. Alternatively, you can recycle large, clean plastic bags for the purpose.

The point of covering the dough is to prevent it from drying out. Shower caps also allow for expansion of the dough in the bowl, and if any escapes, it will be caught in the cap. You could also use a clean, damp tea towel or beeswax wraps.

Rice flour: This is the best flour to line your banneton (see next item) with, to stop the dough from sticking to it; it is easily found in Asian food shops or natural food stores/baking aisles, or you can grind your own uncooked rice to a fine flour.

Banneton or bowl: A banneton is a cane proofing basket that gives dough its shape and concentric lines. If you do not have a banneton, you can line a similarly sized bowl with a dry, clean, lint-free tea towel, making sure to flour it well, and use that to proof the dough in. My standard master recipe and master loaves work perfectly with a banneton 8¾ inches (22 cm) in diameter and 3¼ inches (8.5 cm) deep, or an 11-inch (28-cm)-long oval banneton. Other sizes needed for specific recipes will be referenced in the recipe.

If you have a new banneton that is not already prepared/seasoned, remove any cotton liner, then moisten the interior surface of the banneton with water and sprinkle it all over with rice flour. Tip and tap it all around to ensure that the rice flour covers every internal part of the banneton. Leave it out, uncovered, to dry overnight or for several hours; this will create a crust that is your perfect "nonstick" surface. This needs to be done only once.

Sprinkle extra rice flour inside the banneton before each use.

When you have finished using the banneton, leave it out on the counter to dry out, then store it in a dry cupboard. You do not need to clean it out; it can remain perfectly crusty with its layer of rice flour ready for the next use.

Do not wrap it in plastic as that will cause it to sweat and go moldy.

The only time you need to clean or consider replacing your banneton is if it becomes moldy. And then, it will need a really good scrub and to dry out thoroughly before you use it again.

Roasting pan/pot: For my round loaves, I use a 10¼-inch (26-cm)-diameter round enamel roasting pan with a lid. For my oval loaves, I use an 11¾-inch (30-cm)-long oval enamel roasting pan with a lid, or a 13¾-inch (35-cm)-long clay baker. You can also use a cast-iron Dutch oven or a Le Creuset pan, if you prefer, a carbon steel pan or your choice of baking pan.

I always use a pan with a lid; I prefer enamel roasters as they are lighter than cast-iron pans and also heat up faster and cool down faster. They are relatively inexpensive and last forever.

Baking loaves in a pan with a lid on it captures the steam that comes from the dough as it bakes, which encourages the rise of the dough and formation of the crust.

If you do not have a pan that you can use to bake your loaf in, you can create the same effect by placing the dough on a baking sheet or cookie sheet and inverting a deep baking pan or ovenproof bowl over the dough. A Pyrex dish works well. Ensure that whatever you use allows the dough to grow as it bakes. For safety, make sure that whatever pan and lid you use can withstand temperatures up to 450°F (230°C).

Good-quality parchment baking paper: This is to line the inside of the pan and stop the dough from sticking. Do not use waxed paper; it will stick to your dough.

Oven: While obvious, it is worth noting that I have provided oven temperatures in Fahrenheit and Celsius for convection and conventional ovens. I use a standard domestic oven. I tend to use mine on the convection setting, but it is not a necessity. One key tip is to get to know your oven and, if possible, use a thermometer to check that your temperatures are accurate. If you are having trouble with your loaves, get an oven thermometer; an oven that runs too hot or too cool could be the issue.

Wire cooling rack: You will need one of these to transfer the loaf to, once baked. If you place the freshly baked loaf on a flat surface, the bottom will become soggy from the steam the hot loaf produces.

These are the things that I also use regularly; they are good to have but not essential:

Bread lame for scoring the dough: A lame is a handle that holds a razor blade. You need a razor blade to score your dough; sharp knives are never thin or sharp enough and will drag across the dough.

Bread lames are designed so that you can use all four corners of the blade before needing to replace it. You will be able to tell when the blade needs to be changed: It will start to drag your dough instead of cleanly scoring it.

Please be careful with the blades.

Dough knife/dough scraper or cutter/bench scraper: These are all different terms for the same tool, which is designed for cleanly cutting into dough. My dough knife is nonstick, which is perfect for sourdough, as it can be so sticky.

Bowl scraper/spatula: This can be useful for easing the dough from the bowl when necessary for the recipe.

Flour shaker: A shaker for your rice flour is really useful for not ending up with rice flour all over your kitchen.

Sourdough Starter

Sourdough starter is the yeast element used for making sourdough loaves. It is what gives sourdough its great flavor and texture. Starter is a thick liquid made from flour and water; it may look like a bowl of slop, but that belies the strength within it. Starter is created by allowing the flour and water to ferment over time to cultivate the wild yeast and good bacteria found naturally in the flour and in the air. You cannot see wild yeast, or buy it, but it is something you can grow simply at home. The process of making a starter with flour and water generates the power needed to make sourdough bread.

Time and patience are the hidden ingredients in any sourdough recipe. Unlike working with commercial yeast, it is not a case of opening the pot, mixing it up and producing a loaf in two hours. Sourdough is a slow developer and your starter is what makes that wonderful process happen. It takes time to make and develop your starter, and it will get stronger and gain more flavor the longer you have it and the more you use it.

Your starter is, in essence, a living thing that needs feeding and looking after, which sounds a lot harder than it actually is. Some people view their starter as another member of their family; some worry about looking after it properly; others have been known to take it with them on vacation. But if you follow the instructions in this book, you will see that owning a sourdough starter does not have to mean that your life has to be put on hold. Your starter needs feeding and tending when you want to use it, but other than that, it is stored in the fridge between uses.

HOW TO MAKE A STARTER

Creating a starter is extremely fulfilling; watching the simple mixture of flour and water come alive with activity and bubbles is pure joy. To then see that mixture generate a bowl full of dough, which then bakes into a lovely loaf, feels like magic every time.

Before you begin mixing your first sourdough starter, here are some tips to take into account and help you with the process:

- Sourdough starter is made by mixing flour and water so that the natural wild yeast and good bacteria in the flour ferment; at the same time, the mixture is attracting and benefiting from naturally occurring wild yeast in the air. The more you work with wild yeast, the more you generate, so my kitchen is quite alive with wild yeast from all the sourdough that I mix. If making sourdough is new for you, do not be discouraged if your starter takes more than a week to be ready to use. Stick with it—it will happen.

- A digital scale makes a huge difference when making a starter. Being able to weigh equal amounts of flour and water really help, not only to create the starter, but also when it comes to maintaining it. Everything changed for me when I stopped using cup measures for my starter and started using a digital scale. I have included cup measurements for readers who would rather use them; they do not translate exactly to the weights that I prefer to use, but they will still work fine.

- To be safe, I would advise using water that has been boiled and cooled, or filtered; you can use it at room temperature or cool. Later, you can test your tap water in a small portion of your starter to see whether it can be used.

- If you are new to sourdough, I would highly recommend starting with a good strong white bread flour, which is what these instructions are based on. Information about making starters with other flours follows.

- As you create your starter, keep it somewhere that is not too cold, maybe even a little bit warm, but also not too hot. Sourdough responds to temperature—cold will slow it down; heat will speed it up, but if it becomes too warm, it could then work too fast and risk being spoiled. Between 64°F (18°C) and 68°F (20°C) works perfectly.

- The instructions require one short action per day; this can be done at a time that suits you, around every 24 hours. It does not need to be at exactly the same time every day; you do not need to set a timer.

- When instructed to discard some of the starter, you really do need to discard it. Do not be tempted not to, resulting in too much starter. If you keep too much, you will make your starter slow and sluggish. Many people new to sourdough are tempted not to discard it as they do not have the heart to remove their carefully created starter, but it is a necessary step to build your starter's strength. It only needs to be done a few times; then, after that, no discarding is necessary.

- I use small quantities to make starters. You will therefore have very little waste, but when you do need to discard, put the spare starter in a separate bowl and use it in other recipes. Resist the temptation to keep the excess starter, as you will end up with endless bowls containing small bits of starter.

- I always advocate using any starter you have to discard in a recipe, such as in my biscuits (see pages 107–115) or crackers (pages 175–181), but if you do choose to throw it away, never throw it down the sink or toilet. Sourdough starter dries like concrete and resists water; your drains will not like it.

- Always stir your starter with clean stainless-steel spoons and forks. And always clean them immediately after use; otherwise, the starter will dry on them like a rock.

- Choose a name for your starter; it is all part of the fun!

THE PROCESS

Day 1:
In a glass or ceramic bowl, mix 50 grams (¼ cup) of water with 50 grams (½ cup) of strong white bread flour, or a different flour of your choice.

Stir the mixture well, scrape down the sides of the bowl and mix it all in; it will be nicely thick. Loosely cover the bowl, allowing a slight opening in the lid to attract the natural wild yeast in the air. Leave the bowl on the kitchen counter.

Day 2:
Bubbles may already be starting to appear on the surface of your mixture; it may also be very glutinous and bouncy once fed. If not, that is normal, too. Add 30 grams (¼ cup) of your flour and 30 grams (⅛ cup) of water, stir it well, scraping down the sides of the bowl again and mix it all in (see photos 1, 2 and 3 on the next page), then loosely cover the bowl and leave it on the counter again.

Day 3:
More bubbles should be appearing now and it may be starting to smell interesting. An eggy or cheesy odor is not unusual at this point. Add 30 grams (¼ cup) of your flour and 30 grams (⅛ cup) of water, stir it well, scraping down the sides of the bowl and mix it all in, then loosely cover the bowl and leave on the counter.

Note: Around this time, new starters typically begin to look bubbly and it is really exciting to see; this is the bacteria and yeast doing their work. However, do not be fooled into thinking that your starter is ready to use. It is not strong enough yet; these changes are all part of the life cycle of making a starter. The bubbles will typically subside over the next few days, but then they will return and stay for longer.

Day 4:

Your starter may now be smelling vinegary; that is all normal—it indicates the fermenting process is happening. Discard half of the contents of the bowl. Literally remove half and either throw it in the trash (not the sink) or put it into another bowl, cover it and put it into the fridge to use later, or use it for the biscuit (see pages 107–115) or cracker recipes (see pages 175–181). Add 30 grams (¼ cup) of your flour and 30 grams (⅛ cup) of water, stir well, scrape down the sides of the bowl, then loosely cover the bowl and leave on the counter.

Day 5:

If your starter is now looking less active and bubbly, do not be disheartened; it is all part of the process. Stick with it and keep building the strength in your starter. Add 30 grams (¼ cup) of your flour and 30 grams (⅛ cup) of water, stir well, scrape down the sides of the bowl, then loosely cover the bowl and leave it on the counter.

Day 6:

Discard half of the contents of the bowl. Again, literally remove half of the starter and either throw it in the trash (not down the sink), or put it in the bowl with the other portion of discarded starter, cover it and put it in the fridge to use later or for biscuits or crackers. Add 30 grams (¼ cup) of your flour and 30 grams (⅛ cup) of water, stir well, scraping down the sides of the bowl, then loosely cover the bowl and leave it on the counter.

Day 7:

Hopefully, you are now seeing bubbles all the way through the mixture (see photo 4). White flour starters can look really exciting now—bubbly and even volcanic. Add 30 grams (¼ cup) of your flour and 30 grams (⅛ cup) of water, stir well, scraping down the sides of the bowl, then loosely cover the bowl and leave it on the counter.

IS IT READY TO USE?

By now, your starter could be ready to use. If it is a white flour starter, the consistency should be thick and glutinous; if it is whole wheat or whole grain, it should be wonderfully textured and nicely thick. Once it has been fed and has had time to grow and blossom to double its size, and become fully active, the bubbles and texture should be all the way through the liquid; but if you are not sure, repeat the same process again from Day 2 onward for up to a total of fourteen days from when you started, by which time it should be ready to use.

I assess the readiness of my starter by stirring it, dispersing the bubbles and seeing how quickly and heartily the bubbles come back; when they come back quickly and abundantly, it is ready. If I stir the starter and the bubbles disperse and do not come back immediately, it is not ready. At this point, I would keep building the strength in my starter.

Some things to keep in mind:

- Do not get disheartened if your starter takes longer to be ready; making sourdough is a slow process. It requires time and patience, but it will all be worth the wait.

- Starters also get stronger in power and flavor, the older they get. The more you use them, the better they will get. Read about maintaining and using your starter in the next sections.

Once your starter is established, keep the lid firmly shut tight and store it in the fridge between uses. This puts your starter to sleep while you do not need it. From this point on, you no longer need to keep discarding and feeding; when you are going to use it, feed it as explained in the following sections.

Top Tip:
Always aim to keep a base amount of 100 g of starter only at any time. This is a perfect base amount to keep your starter lean, healthy and active.

Please note that if, at any point during the making or maintaining of it, your starter develops a murky gray liquid across the top, it is fine. Do not worry—it is not ruined, just letting you know that it is hungry. It might have been warmer and so may have worked harder and faster during that period of time, and now it just needs feeding.

You now have two options: You can either stir in the liquid and feed it as usual, or pour it away and feed it as usual.

This liquid is often called "hooch" as it is alcohol produced by overfermentation of the starter mixture; by stirring it in, you help build the flavor of your starter. This does not mean, however, that your starter is now alcoholic. If you are concerned, pour the liquid away and ensure that it does not occur again by keeping a careful eye on your starter and your room temperature.

Changes to your starter that need attention:

- If your starter becomes a thin liquid at any time, feed it flour only and thicken it up, then manage the thickness as you continue making it; it is just responding to its environment. You may need to feed it more flour than water for a few days.

- If your starter develops pink or orange spots, or your jar develops white, black or green furry bits, this is mold; sadly, your starter cannot be saved from this and it should be totally discarded; you will need to start again.

- If your starter develops a hard, dry top layer, it is getting too dry on the top. Scrape off the top layer and keep your starter firmly covered to protect it from now on.

HOW TO MAKE STARTERS USING WHOLE GRAIN AND ANCIENT-GRAIN FLOURS

The process and number of days required to make starters with flours other than strong white bread flour is the same; however, they all differ slightly due to the consistency, texture and strength of each flour.

Exactly the same tips and guidelines apply as previously discussed. One of the main differences when making these starters will be the smell. Especially around Days 3 and 4, they may smell quite bad, but it is all normal; just keep going and the smell will reduce. You may also find that the top layer of the mixture becomes darker than the mixture beneath it; it is all part of the process. Just keep stirring and following the steps.

Any of these starters can be used with any of the recipes in this book; that is, the starters can be directly swapped for one another. Different starters create different flavors and textures in the resultant loaves and are great fun to play with.

Please note that the flour in the dough does not need to match the flour in the starter.

Whole Wheat Flour Starter

I would recommend using a strong whole wheat flour, ideally with a protein content of 13 to 15 percent.

If you use very strong whole wheat flour, initially the starter may look like an elastic blob, resisting the water it is being mixed with. Keep stirring it and following the steps and it will go on to become a beautiful textured bowl of power.

Whole Grain Einkorn Flour Starter

A whole grain einkorn starter can look like a bowl of brown slop, but within that sloppy mixture is the power to lift beautifully risen loaves. When you first mix it, it will look like a paste and it will also resist the water. Keep stirring it regularly; the water will mix in and the starter will become activated.

Whole Grain Emmer Flour Starter

Whole grain emmer flour responds wonderfully for making a starter; it is lively and very active. When first mixed, it will also resist the water, so stir it regularly. Emmer flour quickly becomes a nice bouncy mixture rather than a paste, like einkorn. Emmer produces a wonderful smelling and acting starter.

Spelt Flour Starters

I would highly recommend using whole grain spelt flour, as opposed to white spelt flour, for making a starter. The whole grain version has more texture and strength. These starters are beautifully textured beneath a smooth surface and smell inviting once established.

Whole Grain Khorasan Flour

Whole grain Khorasan flour creates a thick mixture when you use it to make a starter and can look spongy rather than vivaciously bubbly. However, as you stir it, you will see texture and activity beneath a smooth surface. A Khorasan starter generates a firm dough and great flavor.

Whole Grain Dark Rye Flour

Whole grain dark rye flour produces a thick mixture; you may find initially that you need to use 15 grams (1 tablespoon) more water than flour to begin making the starter, then revert to equal weights once it is established.

Whichever flour you choose to make your starter, nurture it and allow it time to develop. And most of all, have fun. Enjoy the process!

HOW TO MAKE A STARTER IN HIGH TEMPERATURES

High temperatures and/or humidity can affect your starter greatly. Both can make your starter work a lot faster, which means it works its way through the flour more quickly and thus can become thin and weak.

Follow all the same notes, tips and timetable for making a starter, but store your new starter in the fridge during the day across the highest temperatures.

Watch and assess how your starter behaves. If at any point the starter is becoming thin or is developing a dark murky liquid on the surface, it is working fast in the heat. Stir it well and feed it only flour until it is back to its previous thickness. You can do this as many times as necessary to maintain the consistency.

HOW TO FEED AND USE YOUR STARTER

When you plan to make some dough, work the timings backward to plan when you need to take your starter from the fridge and when to feed it. See the timetables on page 183 for assistance.

Take your starter from the fridge, let it sit on the counter with its lid on, and let it come up to room temperature (see photo 1 on the next page). Please note that you can feed your starter while cold, but the liquid will be thick and resistant and it will take longer to come up to play.

Once it is at room temperature, it may well start to bubble even before you have fed it—this shows how wonderfully happy and strong it is. Now, feed it with your chosen flour and water.

For a single full-size dough based on my master recipe, feed your starter 30 grams (¼ cup) of flour and 30 grams (⅛ cup) of water (see photo 2 on the next page).

Stir it well (see photo 3 on the next page). You do not need to stir until it is perfectly smooth; it can be lumpy. Your starter will eat through the flour quite happily. Replace the lid firmly and leave it on the counter to work.

Always feed all of your starter; you do not need to separate out a portion for feeding.

The process of "feeding" your starter is doing just that: The additional flour and water provide it with nourishment and energy. As your starter eats its way through this new food, it gains energy and power, which make it bubble and grow. Once it has used up all of the nutrients from the feed, it will become still again and will start to drop back down. Starters do not remain bubbly and active forever, only for a period of time after feeding, just as when we consume a meal, it only nourishes us for a while before we need to eat again.

When it is grown and blossomed, happy, bubbly and active, begin your dough (see photo 4).

By feeding your starter 30 grams (¼ cup) of flour and 30 grams (⅛ cup) of water, it will generate the 50 grams (¼ cup) of the bubbly starter that you need to make your dough; then, when you take into account whatever is stuck to the spoon and you stir down the rest of the starter, it will return it back to your base amount.

Remember: If you ever find that you are building up a larger amount of starter, use some up in another recipe and return it to your perfect base amount. Such recipes as the biscuits (see pages 107–115) or crackers (see pages 175–181) are a great way to use up extra starter.

Tips:

If you want to make multiple loaves, feed it multiples of 30 grams (¼ cup) of flour plus 30 grams (⅛ cup) of water accordingly. For example, to make 2 loaves, I feed my starter 60 grams (½ cup) of flour plus 60 grams (¼ cup) of water; for 3 loaves, I feed it 90 grams (¾ cup) of flour plus 90 grams (scant ½ cup) of water; and so on.

Please note that when you feed your starter more flour and water, it may take longer to become active.

The time your starter takes to be ready to use will depend on the temperature in your kitchen.

If it is cold, well below 64°F (18°C), it will take longer. If it is warmer, well over 68°F (20°C), it will be faster.

If you have sunshine coming into your kitchen, sit your starter in the sunshine for 1 to 2 hours for a boost of heat.

HOW TO BOOST YOUR STARTER

If you feel that your starter has become weak or inactive, you can usually get it back on track very simply. Do not assume it is dead. That is rarely the case, so do not throw it away; try giving it this boost and see what happens:

Twice a day, across 48 hours, remove half of your starter, then feed it 30 grams (¼ cup) of your chosen flour plus 30 grams (⅛ cup) of water and store it at room temperature, firmly covered, for a total of four feedings. Hopefully, you should see quite a difference.

Tips:

Use what you remove to make some flatbreads or pancakes; it will still be full of flavor even if it is not active.

Remember, if you do not already use a strong white bread flour for your starter, I recommend using it now. It can make a massive difference to the activity of your starter.

STARTER FAQS AND TROUBLESHOOTING GUIDE

Before I begin, please let me reassure you that sourdough starters are very resilient. If you follow the guidelines for maintaining it, it will work well. Starters are very hard to kill.

Why is my starter not bubbly?

If your starter is not getting bubbly, it may need a boost, as described previously, or it may need to be fed with stronger flour.

It may also be cold. If the temperatures have dropped where you are, place your starter somewhere a little warmer, ideally around 68°F (20°C) to warm it up, and see how it responds.

It may have already eaten through its feed and reached its peak of activity and become quiet again. Feed it again and watch it carefully.

Why is my starter not growing?

As long as your starter is becoming bubbly and active, it is a happy, healthy starter. It does not need to grow abundantly. Having said that, ensure that you are feeding it a good strong flour and maintaining it as I have described.

Why has my starter got tiny bubbles?

Tiny bubbles mean that your starter is becoming too thin. This will happen if it has become warm, which makes sourdough eat through its flour faster.

Feed it only a portion of flour, 20 to 30 grams (⅛ cup), depending on how thin your starter is, then allow it to respond and bubble. Repeat this if necessary to thicken it up again.

Why does my starter smell weird/bad/gross?

Your starter will have its very own odor—sour, vaguely alcoholic, like eggs or, like mine, paint. Yes, my starter smells like paint, yet it is perfectly healthy.

How much starter should I start with to make the master recipe?

Start with all of it.

Hopefully, you are only keeping around 100 grams (½ cup) of starter, in which case, always feed the entire amount—it helps build the strength of the starter every time you use it this way.

If you maintain more starter than that, still feed the whole amount. It keeps your starter fit and healthy and builds its strength with every use.

Can I feed my starter straight from the fridge?

Yes, though it will be stiffer to stir and will take longer to respond after feeding.

Can I keep my starter at room temperature?

If you are going to use your starter every day, you can keep it out at room temperature. Otherwise, store it in the fridge to stop it from overworking. If you keep it out all the time, you will find yourself having to tend to it daily, which is unnecessary and a waste of flour.

Can I freeze starter?

You can. When you defrost it, you may need to feed and discard some of it several times to bring it back to full strength.

Do I always have to feed my starter the same weights of flour and water?

Yes, as this maintains a happy, healthy liquid starter that will work perfectly.

Can I feed my starter with different flour?

If you want to feed your starter with a different flour to see how it behaves, separate out a portion and feed it with the new flour, but always keep a base amount unadulterated.

I fed my starter to make some dough, but now have to go out—what should I do with it?

Put it back into the fridge and use it later. When you are ready, take it from the fridge, allow it to come up to room temperature and let it finish its feed and bubble up.

I put more than 30 grams (⅛ cup) of water in my starter when feeding it—what do I do?

Feed it with the same weight of flour and stir it well.

What hydration is your starter?

By feeding it equals weights of flour and water, it is deemed a 100% hydration starter. All the recipes in this book use this 100% hydration starter. Even if you choose to use any recipes that call for a different hydration, you can still use this starter.

Welcome to My Master Recipe

This is the process that I follow every week and use as the basis for so many of my sourdough creations. This is based on straightforward, workable, simple actions, keeping the process as easy and efficient as possible. It may look long, but only because I have included as much information as possible to ensure that your path to sourdough success is smooth. Once you have followed the steps a few times, it will become second nature to mix together and bake your dough this way, resulting in great loaves.

The process for making a single loaf can encompass up to 24 hours, but the actual hands-on input required is very little, 30 minutes at most. Before you begin, read through the process and some example baking timetables on page 183 to best plan your bake.

PREP: When you want to bake a loaf, take your starter from the fridge and let it come up to room temperature. Feed your starter with 30 grams (¼ cup) of strong white bread flour and 30 grams (⅛ cup) of filtered, or boiled and cooled, water, and stir it all together well. Cover the vessel firmly and allow it to become fully active and ready to use. This can take two to three hours in temperatures over 68°F (20°C); it may take four hours or more in temperatures lower than 68°F (20°C). This also depends on the activity of your starter; if yours needs longer to be fully active, build that into your planning.

Makes 1 standard loaf

50 g (¼ cup) active starter

350 g (scant 1½ cups) water, cool or at room temperature

500 g (4 cups) strong white bread flour

7 g (1 tsp) salt, or to taste (any granulated salt of your choice)

Materials

Digital scale

Large mixing bowl

Clean shower cap or damp tea towel

Banneton, or bowl

Rice flour, for dusting

Enamel pan or other baking pan with a lid

Parchment paper

Lame or razor blade

THE PROCESS: Starting this process around mid- to late-afternoon works really well, preferably around 4:00 to 5:00 p.m. However, if your starter is ready to use later, there will still be more than enough time to create the dough.

STEP 1: In your large mixing bowl, combine the bubbly starter with the water and loosely stir them together. They do not need to be perfectly mixed, just swished around to stop the starter from sitting on the bottom of the bowl.

Next, add the strong white bread flour and salt. I tend to use less salt than other bakers; if you would prefer to use more, please do.

I initially use a stainless-steel tablespoon or bread whisk to gently start to mix it all together, go in with my hands to give the dough a final few squeezes and then scrape down the bowl. The dough does not need to be handled very much at this point, it does not need to be kneaded, and it does not need to be smooth. The only aim here is to loosely mix the starter and water through the flour.

(Continued)

Cover the bowl with the shower cap and leave it for an hour or so on the kitchen counter. It can sit for 45 minutes, it can sit for 60 minutes, or it can be 90 minutes. If you get busy with something else, it will not spoil your dough.

You do not need to feed any leftover starter again after use; just store it, covered, in the fridge until you need it again for another recipe.

STEP 2: After an hour or so, perform the first set of pulls and folds. This process gives the gluten a workout, stimulates the wild yeast and builds up the structure in the dough. It really does make a difference to your dough.

Tip:

Dip your fingers in water to prevent sticking.

Literally pick up a handful of dough from one side of the bowl, using your thumb and two forefingers to grab a portion, lift it, stretch it and fold it over the rest of the dough to the other side of the bowl; you do not need to pull it too tight. Then, turn the bowl a few degrees and repeat the process—lift and fold, turn the bowl, lift and fold, turn the bowl—and continue until the dough comes together into a smoothish ball. Then stop.

Tips:

At this point, the dough will be at its stickiest. As you work with it, the stickiness will typically start to reduce, depending on your flour.

Far fewer pulls and folds will be required in the next steps to pull the dough into a ball before covering and leaving it again.

Cover the bowl again with the shower cap and leave it out on the kitchen counter. You can now leave the bowl again for an hour, or half an hour, whatever works for you. It does not need to be a specific time; it can fit in with whatever you are doing. This allows the dough time to settle before performing the next set of actions.

STEP 3: Over the next few hours, perform 3 more sets of the lifting and folding action, exactly the same as before, just enough to bring the dough into a ball; this is the dough telling you when it is time to stop. It will probably take only a few pulls and folds to form it into a ball. Again, these do not need to be done at fixed time periods, as long as you fit in sufficient sets during that time to build up the structure of the dough, which is the key. After each set, cover the bowl and leave it on the counter.

Do the final set before going to bed.

Tips:

The dough will not start to grow at this stage, so do not expect it to become bigger with each handling. The ball that you have created will loosen up and the dough will spread to fill the base of the bowl in between each set of pulls and folds. This is normal.

Unlike regular yeast doughs that are left to rise and then punched down, sourdough does not dictate to you when to resume pulling and folding. These actions do not need to be done at certain times apart; you do not need to set a timer or be held prisoner by your dough. If you are making dinner, puttering in and out of the kitchen, going out and coming back, just fit the 3 sets around what works for you.

STEP 4: Replace the shower cap over your bowl and leave it on the counter overnight. This is often termed as the "bulk fermentation" or "bulk proofing" period. Here, I just call it the overnight proofing. I typically let my dough proof, untouched, for 8 to 10 hours.

Tip:
Please note that this works successfully at 64 to 68°F (18 to 20°C). If your overnight room temperature is higher or lower, refer to the tips on pages 22 and 23.

STEP 5: By the next morning, you should have a bowl full of grown dough, which has typically doubled in size. There may or may not be bubbles across the top of your dough; it all depends on what flour you have used, and it is not a requirement. If you have used a glass bowl, you should be able to see bubbles all the way through the dough and it should fill the bowl, assuming you have used a bowl of a size similar to mine, 9 inches (23 cm) in diameter and 3½ inches (9 cm) deep.

You will also notice condensation on the underside of the shower cap as a result of the natural heat and activity that the dough generates.

Next, get out your banneton (see page 14)—mine is 8¾ inches (22 cm) in diameter and 3¼ inches (8.5 cm) deep—and liberally sprinkle it with more rice flour. It needs to be really well floured, even if you have already got your lovely rice flour crust in it, all the way up the sides, so that the dough does not stick. Alternatively, if using a regular bowl, line it with a clean, dry tea towel dusted with rice flour.

Gently perform a single series of lifts and folds of the dough, just once around the bowl, a maximum of about 10 actions, to bring it into

a ball again. The dough should be bouncy and happy, and you will feel a resistance in the dough. You literally could not squash it flat if you tried, but do not try! Do not be heavy handed and do not handle the dough too much, so as to protect the carefully crafted bubbles. All you need to do right now is gently pull it together so that you can maneuver it into the banneton. The aim at this point is to create a slight tension in the dough to create a ball, without crushing the dough.

Once you have pulled it into a ball and you feel that you can handle it successfully, have your banneton ready and close by. Wet your hand, and place your whole hand over the top of the dough, turn the bowl and everything in it gently upside down with your hand still over the dough and let the dough come into the palm of your hand, so that it sits in your hand. If the dough sticks to the base of the bowl, gently pull the bowl away to free it.

Carefully turn the dough back over to place it, smooth side down, in the banneton, so that it sits in the banneton the same way up as it sat in the bowl.

Tip:
Do not slap the dough down into the banneton; you will smash the air out of the bubbles, which will flatten your loaf.

Once the dough is in the banneton, gently ease it away from the sides with your fingertips and ensure that nowhere is sticking down the sides; if it is, sprinkle extra rice flour down the sides of the dough, between it and the banneton. Be sure to sprinkle some rice flour all over the top of the dough, too, to prevent it from sticking to the parchment paper later.

(Continued)

Cover the banneton with the same shower cap that you previously used for the dough, then put the banneton in the fridge for an absolute minimum of 3 hours, up to a maximum of 10. The longer you leave it, the more the flavor will develop and the dough will firm up. This means you can leave it there all day while you are at work, if you need to, or if you are out for the day, and you can then bake it on your return. Again, it means that making sourdough can fit in with you and your life; it does not have to dictate or dominate your day.

This time in the fridge is often called the final proofing. Its dual aims are for the flavor of the dough to develop and for the dough to firm up so that when you turn it out from the banneton into the pan to bake, it does not spread and lose its shape.

Tips:

My fridge temperature is set to 40°F (4°C).

When you later remove your banneton of dough from the fridge, it may or may not have risen. Please note that it does not need to rise at all in the fridge. The growth will happen when it bakes.

STEP 6: When you are ready to bake, you have two choices: to preheat the oven or bake from a cold start.

Baking bread in an oven that has not been preheated may sound like a crazy idea; we are so used to the notion of preheating ovens, it seems impossible that it would work. But I am here to tell you that it does, and it works brilliantly. I bake all my loaves from a cold start. But if the oven has been on already, I bake them from a preheated start.

Starting with a cold oven means that you do not need to plan your bake, plus you do not waste energy and money heating an empty oven. It takes a leap of faith, but it works, whether you use a pan like mine or a heavier cast-iron Dutch oven. It is also great if you have a clay baker that you would like to use for baking your loaves, as you do not need to presoak the clay to protect it from the shock of the heat; it will heat up gently with the oven. The way starting with a cold oven works is that as the oven heats up, the dough benefits from some extra proofing time before it then begins to bake as it reaches the higher temperatures.

If you choose to preheat the oven, preheat it to 425°F (220°C) convection or 450°F (230°C) conventional.

For either method, have an enamel roaster pan ready—mine is a 10¼-inch (26-cm)-diameter enamel pan—or the pan of your choice, with a lid, as well as good-quality parchment paper.

STEP 7: When the oven is ready (or, if you are baking from a cold start, whenever you are ready to bake), remove the cover from the banneton, place your parchment paper over the top of the banneton and place the pan upside down over the top of them both. With one hand under the banneton and one hand on top of the pan, turn it all over together to turn the dough out of the banneton and into the pan. Do not tip the dough into the pan.

You should now have a lovely dome of dough, which holds its shape, decorated with a pattern of concentric flour rings from the banneton.

Tip:

Leave your used banneton on the counter, uncovered, to dry out before placing it back in your cupboard until you need it again. You do not need to brush it out and do not wrap it in any form of plastic covering, which could cause it to become moldy.

(Continued)

After sitting for an hour or so, start the pulls and folds by lifting a small handful of dough.

Fold it across the rest of the dough, tuck it in and repeat the action.

Continue to do the pulls and folds around the bowl, pulling the dough into a ball.

After each set of pulls and folds, cover the bowl again. After the final set, cover the bowl to leave overnight.

The next morning, once the dough has grown and doubled, perform the same pulling and folding action.

Continue the pulls and folds around the bowl to bring the dough into a bouncy ball.

Place the ball of dough gently into your banneton smooth side down, then cover and place it into the fridge.

Unveil your lovely dome of dough and place into your pot.

Score the dough, put the lid on the pot and bake.

Welcome to My Master Recipe (Continued)

STEP 8: With a lame or a clean razor blade, score the top of the dough cleanly and firmly, at a depth of ¼ to ⅜ inch (0.5 to 1.0 cm). Always score from the outside toward the middle of the dome, to encourage growth. See the section Scoring Your Dough on this page for more details. I scored the loaf in the photo on page 26 with my signature star, a five-spoke "asterisk," cutting from the outer edge into the middle with each stroke.

STEP 9: Put the lid on the pan.

If you preheated the oven, bake for 50 minutes, keeping the lid on for the entire time. Leave it to bake—do not be tempted to peek; do not open and close the oven. Resist any urge to do so, as any influx of air will cause the oven temperature to drop.

If you are baking from a cold start, place the pan in the cold oven, turn the temperature to 425°F (220°C) convection or 450°F (230°C) conventional and bake for a total of 55 minutes from the time that you placed the pan in the cold oven, with the lid on the entire time. Note: If you have an older oven that takes a long time to come up to temperature, you may need to bake the loaf for longer to ensure that it is fully baked.

After the 50 to 55 minutes, remove the covered pan from the oven. Open the lid to check the loaf. Baking in a lidded pan produces a golden loaf. When you take the lid off, if you feel that your loaf is looking pale, place it back in the hot oven, in its pan, minus the lid, for 5 to 10 minutes to brown the loaf to the color of your choice.

Once the loaf is golden brown, carefully remove it from the pan, tilt it while still wearing oven gloves to remove the parchment paper from the bottom (keeping the paper to use again next time if it is not too crisp), then transfer the loaf to a wire rack.

Tip:

If baking a baby master loaf, bake for 45 minutes from the time of placing it in the oven, with an optional extra 5 to 10 minutes, if required.

STEP 10: Leave the loaf on its rack to cool completely. Whichever route you took to bake your loaf, once it is cooling, wait at least 1 hour before you slice into it. If you cut into the loaf too soon, it will still be cooking, plus steam will fill all those carefully crafted holes and make the bread gummy.

A perfect plan is to bake loaves in the evening and leave them on a wire rack overnight. By the next morning, they will be perfectly crusty and fresh and ready for breakfast.

Scoring Your Dough

Scoring, or slashing, your dough prior to baking allows the bread to grow in a way that you choose, rather than it cracking at random as it bakes.

Save yourself a lot of trouble by getting a lame or purchasing an inexpensive box of razor blades. Knives are rarely sharp or thin enough for the job and will drag the dough, whereas a razor blade will cut a swift, clean line.

As you become more comfortable with the dough, you can get creative, but initially score a simple X over the top of your dome of dough and watch it unfold in the baked loaf.

This not only allows the dough to grow in a way you have chosen, but by scoring into the middle, you encourage the rise in the middle.

Always score from the outside edge into the middle of the dome. If you score from the middle outward, there will not be enough space for your hand and your lame, so the blade will drag the dough.

Cut cleanly and with purpose, ¼ to ⅜ inch (0.5 to 1.0 cm) into the dough, using the corner of your blade.

If your blade starts to drag, it may need to be replaced, or your dough may be too soft. Please refer to the troubleshooting section (page 40) to see whether that is the case.

Storing Your Loaves

While the loaf is still whole, leave it on its rack to cool completely and until you are ready to cut into it.

Once it has fully cooled, you can store the loaf in a clean linen or cotton bag for 24 to 36 hours to keep the crust crisp and the inside fresh.

Once you have cut into your loaf, you can use the cloth bag again, placing the loaf cut side down inside the bag, or place what is left in plastic bags, expelling as much air as possible and tying them tightly.

Once stored within a plastic bag, the crust will soften and the inside remain soft for a couple of days.

Freezing Sourdough

Sourdough freezes and defrosts perfectly.

Once fully cooled, place fresh loaves in plastic bags and put them into the freezer.

To defrost, remove the bread from the freezer, take it out of the bag, place it on a wire rack and leave it to defrost for several hours. I usually do this last step at night. By the next morning, it will be perfectly crusty, as if fresh.

You can recrisp or refresh a loaf in a warm oven, if necessary, at around 350°F (180°C), for 5 minutes, if you wish. Sometimes sprinkling the loaf with water aids the crispiness.

If you have made rolls, freeze them once cooled and still crusty. To defrost, leave them, uncovered, on a wire rack for 1 to 2 hours and they will defrost as crusty as they baked.

Same-Day Sourdough Master

I love the process of making sourdough; but I also know that sometimes life steps in and has other ideas. The following method enables you to make a loaf in a single day when you would like a loaf faster than the master recipe allows. The key to the success of this process is temperature. Keeping the dough in some warmth for several hours speeds up the fermentation and removes the need to proof overnight. Also, the use of more starter plus warm water in the dough assists in the outcome, as the dough works faster right from the start.

You may find that the flavor in a same-day loaf is not as developed as in a loaf made over a longer period, but it will still be a wonderfully tasty, textured loaf, in fact, if you prefer a less sour loaf, this could be the process for you. I have included my suggested timings; these can be used exactly or as a guide.

PREP: There are two choices for your starter in this recipe: (a) Prepare your starter by feeding it the night before with 60 grams (⅓ cup) of flour and 60 grams (¼ cup) of cold water. Leave it out overnight up to 68°F (20°C) or in the fridge if it will be warmer than that, ready to use in the morning. Or (b) feed it directly from the fridge first thing in the morning with 60 grams (⅓ cup) of flour and 60 grams (¼ cup) of warm water and put it in a warm place to become active for 1 to 2 hours.

In addition to beginning your starter, prepare a round banneton or bowl with rice flour (see page 14) and set aside a large baking pan with a lid, plus parchment paper.

Makes 1 standard loaf

100 g (½ cup) active starter

325 g (1⅓ cups) warm water, warm to the touch, not hot

300 g (2½ cups) strong white bread flour

200 g (1⅔ cups) whole wheat or strong whole grain flour

7 g (1 tsp) salt, or to taste

9:30 A.M. / STEP 1: In your mixing bowl, combine all the ingredients, stirring them well initially and finishing off by giving the dough a few good squeezes. The dough may be sticky due to the warm water and extra starter. Leave it roughly mixed.

Cover the bowl with a clean shower cap or cover of your choice and place it in a warm spot in your kitchen or home.

You can use the oven with only the oven light on and its door propped open. With my oven, this provides a constant temperature of 77°F (25°C). (If I close the door, that goes up to 99°F (37°C), which is far too hot, even for the shortened proofing time.) If you have a proofing box or warming drawer, that would be ideal for the job. Use a thermometer to monitor the temperature and make sure it does not exceed 77°F (25°C).

10:00 A.M. / STEP 2: Perform the first set of pulls and folds on the dough to build up its structure and stimulate the yeast: Pick up a small handful of the dough, pull it up and across the dough, turn the bowl slightly and repeat the action, all the way around the bowl, several times. It may require more than normal handling at this point due to the stickiness of the dough. Perform the pulls and folds 20 to 25 times.

Cover the bowl again and place it back in the warmth.

10:30 A.M. / STEP 3: Perform the next set of pulls and folds, repeating the same actions again; the dough should be nice and stretchy and bouncy, and it should come together into a nice smooth soft ball.

Place the covered bowl back in the warmth.

11:00 A.M. / STEP 4: Perform the last set of pulls and folds; the dough should come together into a nice, smooth, bouncy ball.

Place the covered bowl back in the warmth for the next 3 hours.

2:00 P.M. / STEP 5: By now, the dough should have grown to at least double its original size. It may be soft from the warm proofing, but it should not be floppy.

Using the same action as for the earlier pulls and folds, pull the dough gently together into a soft, bouncy ball. Do not be heavy handed at this point; handle the dough gently to protect the work your starter has done.

Place the soft, bouncy dough, smooth side down, in your banneton, adding extra rice flour around it if necessary to ensure it is not sticking anywhere, as well as across the top.

Cover the banneton with the same shower cap and place it in the fridge.

5:00 P.M. / STEP 6: Preheat the oven to 425°F (220°C) convection or 450°F (230°C) conventional.

Once the oven is ready, take the banneton from the fridge, remove the cover, place a piece of parchment paper over the top of the banneton, place your pan upside down over the top of both, then turn the banneton and pan over all together to turn out the dough into your pan.

The dough will be softer than usual, so score it with a bread lame or razor blade simply and swiftly. Put the lid on the pan and bake for 50 minutes. If the loaf is still pale after this time, return the pan to the oven, minus the lid, for 5 minutes.

STEP 7: Once baked, carefully remove the loaf from the pan, saving the parchment paper for next time, and allow the loaf to cool on a wire rack for at least an hour before slicing.

Top Tip:
If you like this process, apply the steps to some of the other recipes in this book.

Super Lazy Sourdough Master

If you do not have the time to perform several sets of pulls and folds on the dough, this process cuts out some of the work. The baked loaf may differ slightly from a loaf made with the full set of actions, but only in looks and texture; it will still taste wonderful.

PREP: Feed all of your starter 30 grams (¼ cup) of flour and 30 grams (⅛ cup) of water, and let it sit until active and bubbly. You can also use unfed starter, as long as it has been fed within the previous few days. When ready to make the dough, prepare a banneton or bowl with rice flour (see page 14) and set aside a large baking pan with a lid, plus parchment paper.

Makes 1 standard loaf

50 g (¼ cup) active starter

330 g (1⅓ cups) warm water

500 g (4 cups) strong white bread flour

7 g (1 tsp) salt, or to taste

STEP 1: In the evening, in a large mixing bowl, roughly mix together all the ingredients. Cover the bowl with a clean shower cap or your choice of cover, and leave it on the counter for 30 minutes.

STEP 2: Perform a set of pulls and folds for 4 to 5 minutes, or until the dough is bouncy and starting to form a smooth ball (it will be sticky). Cover the bowl again and leave it on the counter overnight, typically for 8 to 10 hours, at 64 to 68°F (18 to 20°C).

STEP 3: In the morning, the dough should have at least doubled in size. Have your prepared banneton ready and more rice flour at hand. Gently perform a final set of pulls and folds to pull the dough into a ball and carefully place the dough, smooth side down, in the banneton. Sprinkle extra rice flour across the top of the dough and down the sides. Cover the banneton and place it in the fridge for 3 to 10 hours.

STEP 4: When ready to bake, preheat the oven to 425°F (220°C) convection or 450°F (230°C) conventional and have your parchment paper and pan ready. For how to bake from a cold start, visit page 30.

When the oven is ready, place the parchment paper over the top of the banneton and the pan upside down over the top of them both. With one hand under the banneton and one hand on the pan, turn it all over together to turn the dough out of the banneton and into the pan.

Score the dome of the dough. Place the lid on the pan and bake for 50 minutes. After 50 minutes, if you would like more color on your loaf, place the pan back in the oven, minus the lid, for 5 to 10 minutes.

STEP 5: Once baked, carefully remove the loaf from the pan, saving the parchment paper for next time, and allow the baked loaf to cool on a wire rack for at least an hour before slicing.

Sourdough Success

THE UNWRITTEN INGREDIENT

The weather is possibly THE key threat to sourdough. Understanding how weather and temperatures affect sourdough and its progress will help your sourdough journey immensely.

It is simpler than it might sound; cold slows sourdough down, heat speeds it up.

When the ambient temperature drops well below 64°F (18°C), you will find that your starter will take longer to become active and your dough will take longer to proof. You might find that each needs a little warmth, but resist the temptation to leave them somewhere too warm, or for too long, that you overdo it. Better to have your dough underproofed and in need of a helping hand, than overproofed and ruined.

TOP TIPS

To boost your starter in cold weather: Place your fed starter in your oven, with just its light on, for an hour or so, to give it a boost of some warmth. Make sure that you keep an eye on it so that it does not get too hot and become thin and inactive. An oven thermometer is very helpful for this.

To boost your dough in cold weather: If you have proofed your dough overnight but it has been cold and the dough has not grown and doubled, this will result in a heavy loaf with large, uneven holes. If this is the case, give your dough 2 to 3 hours in the oven, with its light on and the door open 6 inches (15 cm). Note that the door must be open. Do not leave the light on and the door shut for several hours, as the oven will get too hot and your dough will overproof.

As an example, inside my oven with just the light on, it gets up to 99°F (37°C). With the door open, it gets up to just 77°F (25°C). Your oven might be different; if you have an oven thermometer, it is worth checking.

Always put a big note on the oven so no one turns it on! Alternatively, hang a towel on the edge of the open door to remind you.

If you have a radiator or other warm place to leave your dough or starter near, do so but watch the temperature carefully, do not keep either too close for too long.

When temperatures rise well above 68°F (20°C), your starter is at risk of working through its feed quickly and becoming thin and inactive. And your dough is at risk of overproofing, so be sure to test the temperature.

In high temperatures: The simplest way to protect your dough is to use a much smaller amount of starter than usual but keep everything else you do the same. I suggest using just 20 grams (⅛ cup) of starter with my standard master doughs and then you will still be able to proof it on the counter overnight.

Make a note, throughout the year, of the times and temperatures and how your starter and dough have behaved and where in the house they have been placed, to build yourself a useful reference.

FAQs AND TROUBLESHOOTING GUIDE

The following section will assist you with my master recipe, as well as with all of the recipes that follow in this book. Before anything else, my biggest and most passionate advice is: Resist the temptation to overthink when making sourdough. It is very easy to do. Sourdough is a truly simple treasure and the more simply you approach it, the better the outcome. Relax and enjoy it! Let the sourdough joy envelop you.

How can I make my loaves more sour?

There are several ways to enhance the sourness of sourdough loaves; for example, a long final proof will help develop the flavor more; once you have mastered making a loaf, try leaving the dough in the fridge for 24 hours before baking, to see the difference the extra time makes to the flavor. Still bake the dough directly from the fridge.

Using a whole grain or rye starter, or including a portion of a whole grain flour in the dough will also enhance the flavor.

Replacing some of the water in your dough with natural plain yogurt can enhance the flavor. Adding peanut butter to the dough makes it really sour; see the recipe on page 73.

How can I make my loaves less sour?

Shortening the final proof time can reduce the sourness. Also, using a young or a stiff starter can help.

A stiff starter is fed with more flour than water, resulting in a much more solid consistency. To do this, feed your starter as normal, then remove 50 grams (¼ cup) of starter and place it in a new bowl. Feed this portion 30 grams (¼ cup) of flour and 15 grams (1 tablespoon) of water over a couple of feeds; it will be like a mini dough and will sponge as it grows. This is now a stiff starter. Use it in exactly the same way as a liquid starter.

By using a portion of your usual starter in this way, you protect your original starter and keep it in your usual base proportions.

How do I make my loaf crusty?

Baking dough in a covered pan helps it to develop a good crust.

If the crust softens once baked and cooling, let it sit on its wire rack for several hours and the crust will crisp up as it cools.

How do I soften the crust?

When you remove the baked loaf from your pan and place it on a wire rack to cool, wrap it in a clean tea towel. This will trap the steam and soften the crust.

How can I soften the crumb of my bread?

Replacing some of the water in the dough with oil or milk will produce a soft interior. Try replacing 30 grams (⅛ cup) of water with an oil of your choice, or half of the water with milk.

Can I shorten the process?

Sourdough needs time. It is a slow mover and needs many hours to truly develop and proof. If you want to reduce the time required to make loaves, follow the master recipe all the way through to the morning after the overnight proofing. Follow the process of putting the dough into the banneton, then place the banneton in the freezer for 45 minutes maximum.

After 45 minutes, turn out the dough into your pan, then score and bake it while still cold, in a preheated oven or with a cold oven start.

This will reduce some of the final process time.

For a same-day version of the recipe, see page 34.

Why has my loaf not risen?

If your loaf has not risen during baking, there could be several reasons.

Your starter may not be strong enough yet. If you feel your starter is healthy and active, then the flour you have used to make the dough may not be strong enough for the loaf to hold its shape.

The dough may also be underproofed and not fully developed, or overproofed and has lost its integrity.

Refer back to the information about flour (see page 11), proofing (see page 29) and room temperature (pages 22–23).

Why is my dough sticky?

Some dough is sticky due to the flour(s) it has been made with, particularly rye flour. I have included notes in recipes where a dough will be sticky. If the dough is firm but sticky, it will be okay.

Alternatively, it could be because your dough is too wet. Different flours work better with different amounts of water. Next time, try reducing the amount of water in your dough by 30 grams (⅛ cup).

The last reason dough can be sticky is that it may have overproofed.

Why does my dough stick to the banneton?

This could be either because your banneton was insufficiently prepared with rice flour (see page 14), your dough is too wet from too much water in it or the dough was overproofed.

Why does my dough spread when I turn it out or when I bake it?

Dough may spread when you turn it out from the banneton for several reasons: Your flour may not have been strong enough, or you may not have built enough structure in the dough with your pulls and folds. Check the type of flour you are using and ensure that you generate enough strength in the dough during the pulls and folds.

It may be because the dough is too wet. Try using 30 grams (⅛ cup) less water next time.

It may be because the dough has overproofed. Check your overnight temperature and ensure that it has not been too warm for the dough.

Why am I unable to score my dough?

See the previous question; the same reasons might apply.

If you feel that you have done everything to build up your dough but still struggle to score it smoothly, place the banneton of dough in your freezer for 30 minutes prior to baking. When you are ready to bake, turn out the dough into your pan, and score and bake immediately. It does not need to warm up again. Also, make sure you are using a lame or razor blade. I have found that kitchen knives do not work well for scoring.

How do you create more "oven spring"?

Oven spring refers to how your dough grows and bursts during the bake. This power is generated by beginning with a good strong starter, using the best flour for your dough and building a good structure in the dough by performing the pulls and folds, which gets the gluten in the flour working to stimulate your starter.

Scoring the dough to encourage growth also helps the loaf grow.

Why is my loaf dense and gummy?

This can be the result of overproofing. The dough loses any strength and bakes flat and dense.

Or it could just be that you need to use less water.

How can I tell whether my dough is overproofed?

If your dough is producing a lot of bubbles, it might be too warm where you are, which will result in your dough working too quickly, putting it at risk of overproofing. Keep an eye on the room temperature if this is the case and move it somewhere cooler.

If, after the main overnight proofing, your dough turns to soup when you touch it, or has no structure whatsoever and is impossible to shape or do anything with, it has overproofed. This will be the result of the overnight temperature being too high.

Either use it for flatbreads or whisk in some milk and use it for pancakes.

How can I tell whether my dough is underproofed?

If, after the main bulk proof, your dough has not at least doubled, it is as risk of being underproofed. This may happen if your starter is not strong enough, or it was cold overnight. See page 23 for the notes about how cold weather can impact your starter and dough.

Why does my loaf have big, uneven holes?

This is typically the result of the dough being underproofed, so it could not bake evenly. See the previous answer.

Do I need to preheat my pan?

No, you do not need to preheat your pan. I never do, and even if you have a cast-iron Dutch oven, it is not necessary. See page 30 for how to bake from a cold oven.

How can I stop my loaf from having a burnt or dark base?

If you find that your loaves are having a very dark and tough bottom, it will be due to your oven and uneven heat.

There are several things that you can try to prevent it:

- Place a baking sheet or cookie sheet on a rack lower down the oven, to disperse the heat away from the base of your dough.

- Place your baking pan on a baking stone.

- Place foil underneath the parchment paper inside your pan.

- Place a good layer of rice flour underneath your parchment paper inside your pan.

- Or try a mix of one or two of these options.

I have mixed my dough but suddenly need to go out; what do I do?

If you will be away for only a few hours, cover the bowl and leave it out at room temperature; you can then return to it and continue working with it when you return. If you will be away for longer, place the bowl in the fridge. Allow it to come up to room temperature before beginning to work with it again.

My dough is in the banneton and in the fridge but an emergency has come up; what do I do?

As long as your dough is strong enough, it can remain in the banneton and in the fridge for up to three days before it is baked. Some people have even left it for longer and the dough has still baked successfully. Never assume all is lost with sourdough; it always surprises.

I forgot to add salt to my dough; what can I do?

You can add the salt during any of the pulls and folds, or if you have forgotten it completely, enjoy the bread with some salted butter.

Can I mix the dough with a stand mixer?

I always prefer to make my dough by hand, and my recipe does not require heavy kneading, so if you finding kneading an issue, my method is ideal for you.

If you prefer to use a stand mixer, use only a low setting and a few pulses for the first mix of the dough, then perform the pulls and folds by hand.

THE MASTER
at Work

The following recipes are all variations on my master recipe, using varying quantities of whole grains and ancient grains. Some include seeds, nuts or oats; some include whole cooked grains; some have other added ingredients; and all are designed to create great flavors and textures. My master recipe can be the basis for whatever loaf you wish to create, the dough is eminently versatile, providing a wealth of opportunity and fun with your sourdough. As you gain experience with these recipes, you will be able to mix and match and swap flours and ingredients to create your own wonderful loaves.

Please refer back to the "Welcome to My Master Recipe" chapter (page 27) for the full detailed process, hints, tips and assistance.

Tip:
See page 52 to see step-by-step photos of how to pull dough together for an oval banneton.

The 50% Whole Wheat Master

Making sourdough with whole wheat flour not only brings the goodness from the whole grain, but also enhances the flavor of the loaf. You may even notice that the sour flavor is increased. And when you mix whole wheat flour with white bread flour, it produces a wonderfully strong dough and a lovely tasty loaf. The dough will be satisfyingly firm to work with, and to score when the time comes.

For a variation on this recipe, try using white spelt flour (see Notes). White spelt flour is milled spelt with the bran and wheat germ sifted out; it is soft and fine and a perfect partner for heavier flours, such as whole wheat, to lift and lighten the loaf. The depth of flavor this dough produces in the baked loaf is almost indescribable, it is so good.

PREP: Feed all of your starter with 50 grams (½ cup) of flour and 50 grams (¼ cup) of water. Once it is active and bubbly and ready to use, begin your dough. Prep a round banneton or bowl with rice flour (see page 14) and set aside a large baking pan with a lid, plus parchment paper.

Makes 1 standard loaf

75 g (⅜ cup) active starter

350 g (scant 1½ cups) water

250 g (2 cups) strong white bread flour

250 g (2 cups) whole wheat flour

7 g (1 tsp) salt, or to taste

STEP 1: In the early evening, in a large mixing bowl, roughly mix together all the ingredients, leaving the dough shaggy, and cover the bowl with a clean shower cap or your choice of cover. Let the dough sit on the counter for 2 hours.

STEP 2: After the 2 hours, perform the first set of pulls and folds on the dough. It may start off being quite sticky, but it will become less so the more you work with it, and it will eventually come together into a ball, which is the perfect time to stop. Cover the bowl again and leave it on the counter.

STEP 3: Over the next few hours, perform 3 more sets of pulls and folds on the dough, covering the bowl of dough after each set, doing the final set before going to bed. The dough will become beautifully stretchy as you work with it and will come together into a soft ball each time.

STEP 4: Leave the covered bowl on the counter overnight, typically 8 to 10 hours, at 64 to 68°F (18 to 20°C).

STEP 5: In the morning, the dough should have doubled, possibly even slightly more than doubled, with a smooth slightly bubbly surface.

Have your prepared banneton ready and more rice flour at hand. Gently perform a final set of pulls and folds to pull the dough into a ball, then carefully place the dough smooth side down in the banneton.

Sprinkle extra rice flour across the top of the dough and down the sides to ensure it is not sticking. Cover the bowl with the same shower cap and place it in the fridge for at least 3 hours.

STEP 6: After 3 to 10 hours in the fridge, when you are ready to bake, preheat the oven to 425°F (220°C) convection or 450°F (230°C) conventional. For how to bake from a cold start, see page 30.

Remove the cover from the banneton, then place the parchment paper over the top of the banneton and the pan upside down over the top of them both. With one hand under the banneton and one on the pan, turn it all over together to turn the dough out of the banneton and into the pan.

Using a bread lame or razor blade, score the dough. Place the lid on the pan and bake for 50 minutes. After 50 minutes, if you would like more color on your loaf, place the pan back in the hot oven, minus the lid, for 5 to 10 minutes.

STEP 7: Once baked, carefully remove the loaf from the pan, saving the parchment paper for next time, and allow the baked loaf to cool on a wire rack for at least an hour before slicing.

Notes:

The loaf in the photo is my whole wheat and white spelt master loaf, scored with a single arc off center before being baked.

For the whole wheat and white spelt master, feed all of your starter according to the main recipe, then use the following ingredients:

50 g (¼ cup) active starter
350 g (scant 1½ cups) water
250 g (2¼ cups) white spelt flour
250 g (2 cups) whole wheat flour
7 g (1 tsp) salt, or to taste

The Whole Wheat and All-Purpose Einkorn Oval Master

These flours make a perfect partnership for use with my master recipe. The flavors complement each other and the lighter all-purpose einkorn flour evens out the heavier whole wheat flour. The dough bakes to a fabulously crusty textured loaf! All the master doughs can be baked as round or oval loaves. I have baked this one as an oval to show that option.

PREP: Feed your whole starter with 50 grams (½ cup) of flour and 50 grams (¼ cup) of water. Once it is active and bubbly and ready to use, begin your dough. Prepare your banneton or a bowl with rice flour (see page 14) and set aside a large baking pan with a lid, plus parchment paper.

Makes 1 standard loaf

75 g (⅜ cup) active starter

375 g (1½ cups) water

300 g (2½ cups) whole wheat flour

200 g (1¾ cups) all-purpose einkorn flour

7 g (1 tsp) salt, or to taste

Tip:

Visit page 52 to see step-by-step photos of how to pull the dough together for an oval banneton.

STEP 1: In the evening, in your mixing bowl, roughly mix together all the ingredients. Cover the bowl with a clean shower cap or your choice of cover and leave the dough to sit on the counter for 2 hours.

STEP 2: After the 2 hours, start building the dough by doing the first set of pulls and folds until the dough comes together into a ball. This dough will be quite stretchy, possibly sticky, but will form a firm ball. Cover the bowl again and leave it on the counter.

STEP 3: After another hour or so and over the next few hours, perform 3 more sets of pulls and folds on the dough, covering the bowl after each set. Perform the final set prior to going to bed. The dough may start to be a bit spongy and will be easier to work with on each handling.

STEP 4: Cover the bowl and leave the dough on the counter overnight, typically 8 to 10 hours, at 64 to 68°F (18 to 20°C).

STEP 5: In the morning, the dough should have doubled and have a smooth surface.

To place the dough in the oval banneton, using the same pulling and folding action, lift a small handful of dough from one side of the bowl and pull it across to the middle of the dough. Repeat this action again, from the same side of the bowl, in a line, then turn the bowl 180 degrees and repeat the action from the other side, to create a fat sausage of dough.

(Continued)

Put your whole hand over the dough, turn the bowl over and let the dough come into your hand, then gently turn the dough back over and place it, smooth side down, in the banneton. Sprinkle some extra rice flour down the sides and across the top of the dough, then cover the banneton with the same shower cap and place it in the fridge for at least 3 hours.

STEP 6: After 3 to 10 hours in the fridge, when you are ready to bake, preheat the oven to 425°F (220°C) convection or 450°F (230°C) conventional. For how to bake from a cold start, see page 30.

Remove the cover from the banneton, then place the parchment paper over the top of the banneton and the pan upside down over the top of them both. With one hand under the banneton and one on the pan, turn it all over together to turn the dough out of the banneton and into the pan. The dough will be quite firm.

Using a bread lame or razor blade, score the dough. I scored the loaf in the picture with a single long cut along one of the edges created by the banneton, plus some smaller cuts along the other side.

Put the lid on the pan and bake for 50 minutes. After 50 minutes, if you would like more color on your loaf, place the pan back in the hot oven, minus the lid, for 5 to 10 minutes.

STEP 7: Once baked, carefully remove the loaf from the pan, saving the parchment paper for next time, and allow the baked loaf to cool on a wire rack for at least an hour before slicing.

Note:

The nature of whole grain flours is such that they take longer to absorb water than white flour, but they may soak up more water than white flours. Consequently, for some of the doughs made with more whole wheat/whole grain flour (such as this one and the 100% Whole Wheat Master, page 54), I use more water and slightly more starter. The dough will still typically feel stiffer than a white-only dough and tends to produce a denser loaf. It may also not rise as much as a white loaf, but that is all normal; it will taste great.

The Wonderfully White Spelt Poppy Seed Oval Master

Poppy seeds are a great addition to dough. They look great throughout the baked loaf, as well as taste good. Personally, I prefer putting poppy seeds into dough rather than over the top as it saves getting the kitchen covered in them! This is also a great loaf for an introduction to using ancient grains, as it includes white spelt flour.

White spelt flour is wonderfully soft and very tasty, but benefits from being mixed with a stronger flour to give it support, as is done here. The addition of poppy seeds also adds stability to the loaf.

I have made this loaf in an 11-inch (28-cm)-long oval banneton, but it can also be made as a round loaf. To bake, use an 11¾-inch (30-cm)-long oval pan, or a 13¾-inch (35-cm)-long clay baker lined with parchment paper and bake from a cold start.

PREP: Feed all of your starter with 30 grams (¼ cup) of flour and 30 grams (⅛ cup) of water. Once it is active and bubbly and ready to use, begin your dough. Prepare your banneton or a bowl with rice flour (see page 14) and set aside your lidded pan of choice, plus parchment paper.

Makes 1 standard loaf

50 g (¼ cup) active starter

350 g (scant 1½ cups) water

300 g (2½ cups) strong white bread flour

200 g (1¾ cups) white spelt flour

25 g (⅛ cup) poppy seeds

7 g (1 tsp) salt, or to taste

STEP 1: In the early evening, in a large mixing bowl, roughly mix together all the ingredients, leaving the dough shaggy. Cover the bowl with a clean shower cap or your choice of cover and leave it to sit for 1 hour.

STEP 2: After an hour, begin the first set of pulls and folds on the dough. You will be able to feel the poppy seeds in the dough, and they will help it come together into a ball quite quickly. Cover the bowl again and leave it on the counter.

STEP 3: Over the next few hours, complete 3 more sets of pulls and folds on the dough, until it comes together into a ball each time, covering the bowl after each set. Do the last set of pulls and folds before going to bed.

STEP 4: Leave the covered bowl on the counter overnight, typically 8 to 10 hours, at 64 to 68°F (18 to 20°C).

(Continued)

STEP 5: In the morning, the dough should have grown, ideally slightly more than double its original size. To pull the dough together to be placed into an oval banneton, gently but firmly use the same pulling and folding action and pull 4 to 5 small handfuls of the dough into the middle of the dough in a line. Turn the bowl 180 degrees and repeat the actions to bring the dough into a bouncy fat sausage.

Place your whole hand over the dough, turn the bowl over and let the dough fall into your hand, then place it, smooth side down, in the banneton.

Cover the banneton again with the same shower cap and place it in the fridge for at least 3 hours.

STEP 6: After 3 to 10 hours in the fridge, when you are ready to bake, preheat the oven to 425°F (220°C) convection or 450°F (230°C) conventional. For how to bake from a cold start, see page 30.

Remove the cover from the banneton, then place the parchment paper over the banneton and the pan upside down over the top of them both. With one hand under the banneton and one on the pan, turn it all over together to turn the dough out of the banneton and into the pan.

Using a bread lame or razor blade, score the dough. I scored the loaf in the photo with one single long cut, about ⅜ inch (1 cm) deep, along one side of the flat top created by the banneton. Place the lid on the pan and bake for 50 minutes. After 50 minutes, if you would like more color on your loaf, place the pan back in the hot oven, minus the lid, for 5 to 10 minutes.

STEP 7: Once baked, carefully remove the loaf from the pan, saving the parchment paper for next time if it is not too crisp, and allow the baked loaf to cool on a wire rack for at least an hour before slicing.

The 100% Whole Wheat Master

A completely whole wheat dough is a joy to work with; it becomes spongy yet stretchy as it develops and provides a lovely firm dough.

The loaf will rise less and produce a denser crumb than other loaves, but it will taste fabulous. This dough includes slightly more starter and water to allow for the nature of the flour, which can soak up moisture. Aim to use a whole wheat flour with 13 to 14 percent protein.

PREP: Feed your entire starter 60 grams (½ cup) of flour and 60 grams (¼ cup) of water. Once it is active and bubbly and ready to use, begin your dough. Prepare a round banneton or bowl with rice flour (see page 14) and set aside a large baking pan with a lid, plus parchment paper.

Makes 1 standard loaf

75 g (⅜ cup) active starter

400 g (1⅔ cups) water

500 g (4 cups) whole wheat flour

7 g (1 tsp) salt, or to taste

STEP 1: In the early evening, in a large mixing bowl, roughly mix all the ingredients together, cover the dough with a clean shower cap or your choice of cover and let it sit on the counter for 2 hours. It will already be a soft, spongy mix.

STEP 2: After the 2 hours, perform the first set of pulls and folds until the dough comes together into a nice ball. The dough will be stretchy and spongy and nice to work with. Cover the bowl and leave it on the counter.

STEP 3: Perform 3 more sets of pulls and folds on the dough over the next few hours, covering the bowl after each set, doing the final set prior to going to bed. With each set of pulls and folds, the dough will become softer and stretchier, and slightly spongy as it grows. It will not take many actions to pull the dough into a ball on each occasion.

STEP 4: Cover and leave the bowl on the counter overnight, typically 8 to 10 hours, at 64 to 68°F (18 to 20°C).

STEP 5: In the morning, the dough should have doubled, if not more, with an almost smooth surface. Use the same pulling and folding action to now pull the dough into a ball. It will be firm and spongy, with very little handling required to pull it into a nice firm ball.

Place it, smooth side down, in the banneton; cover the banneton with the same shower cap and place it in the fridge for at least 3 hours. The dough may seem to deflate slightly as you handle it, but fear not, it will grow back during the next phase of its development.

STEP 6: After 3 to 10 hours in the fridge, when you are ready to bake, preheat the oven to 425°F (220°C) convection or 450°F (230°C) conventional. For how to bake from a cold start, see page 30.

Remove the cover from the banneton, then place the parchment paper over the banneton and the pan upside down over the top of them both. With one hand under the banneton and one on the pan, turn it all over together to turn the dough out of the banneton and into the pan.

The dough will be a lovely firm dome and a joy to score. Put the lid on the pan and bake for 50 minutes. After 50 minutes, if you would like more color on your loaf, place the pan back in the hot oven, minus the lid, for 5 to 10 minutes.

STEP 7: Once baked, carefully remove the loaf from the pan, saving the parchment paper for next time, and allow the baked loaf to cool on a wire rack for at least an hour before slicing.

The Light Rye Master

Rye flour tastes great, but it can be quite challenging. It does not become a stretchy dough, and throughout the process, it remains very sticky. You may wish to begin using rye flour in your dough in a smaller portion than suggested in this recipe to see how it feels and behaves, and then build up to a larger amount. But if you do decide to go for it, enjoy the beautifully baked outcome and know that if your dough is sticky and heavy, it is normal. Wetting your hands to handle the dough will prevent it from sticking to you too much.

PREP: Feed all of your starter 50 grams (½ cup) of flour and 50 grams (¼ cup) of water. Once it is active and ready to use, begin your dough. Prepare a round banneton or bowl with rice flour (see page 14) and set aside a large baking pan with a lid, plus parchment paper.

Makes 1 standard loaf

75 g (⅜ cup) active starter

325 g (1⅓ cups) water

350 g (2¾ cups) strong white bread flour

150 g (1½ cups) light rye flour

7 g (1 tsp) salt, or to taste

STEP 1: In the early evening, in a large mixing bowl, roughly mix together all the ingredients into a shaggy dough. Cover the bowl with a clean shower cap or your choice of cover. Let it sit on the counter for 1 hour.

STEP 2: After an hour or so, perform the first set of pulls and folds. You will probably find that the dough is sticky, but it should be stretchy, too. If it is too sticky, it may be easier to fold the dough in on itself, over and over, until it comes together into a still sticky but firm ball. Cover the bowl again and leave it on the counter.

STEP 3: Over the next few hours, complete 3 more sets of pulls and folds on the dough, covering the bowl after each set. Now that the dough has had time to sit, it will start to be easier to stretch. By the third handling, the dough will still be sticky but also stretchy, and possibly starting to feel a bit bouncy; it will come together into a smooth ball. It will also become easier to stretch and maneuver with each handling.

STEP 4: Perform the final set of pulls and folds before going to bed, cover the bowl and leave it on the counter overnight, typically 8 to 10 hours, at 64 to 68°F (18 to 20°C).

STEP 5: In the morning, you should be greeted by a dough that is double in size, nice and grown in your bowl, with a smooth surface.

(Continued)

Perform one last set of pulls and folds to pull it into a ball. The dough may well seem to deflate as you handle it; it may also be a sticky heavy mess. Pull it into a ball as best as you can. Wet your hand and place your whole hand over the ball of dough, turn the whole bowl over and let the dough fall into your hand; you may need to ease it from the bowl firmly if it has stuck. Now, place it gently in the banneton. Cover the banneton again with the same shower cap and place it in the fridge for at least 3 hours.

STEP 6: After 3 to 10 hours in the fridge, when you are ready to bake, preheat the oven to 425°F (220°C) convection or 450°F (230°C) conventional. For how to bake from a cold start, see page 30.

Remove the cover from the banneton, then place the parchment paper over the banneton and the pan upside down over the top of them both. With one hand under the banneton and one on the pan, turn it all over together to turn the dough out of the banneton and into the pan.

Using your bread lame, score the firm dome of dough cleanly. I scored my loaf with a 5-pointed star. Put the lid on your pan and bake for 50 minutes. After 50 minutes, if you would like more color on your loaf, place the pan back in the hot oven, minus the lid, for 5 to 10 minutes.

STEP 7: Once baked, carefully remove the loaf from the pan, saving the parchment paper for next time, and allow the baked loaf to cool on a wire rack for at least an hour before slicing.

The Pumpkin Seed–Crusted Spelt Master

Spelt flour is a joy. It tastes wonderful and smells amazing in your bakes. It is a soft flour, not a strong one, and will make the dough softer. I have slightly reduced the amount of water in the dough to allow for this.

Creating a pumpkin seed crust not only looks impressive but adds more flavor as the seeds toast while the loaf bakes. Adding the seeds prior to putting the dough into the banneton helps them stick to the dough and stops the dough from sticking to the banneton, too, so it is a win-win!

PREP: Feed all of your starter 30 grams (¼ cup) of flour and 30 grams (⅛ cup) of water. Once it is active and ready to use, begin your dough. Prepare a round banneton or bowl with rice flour (see page 14) and set aside a large baking pan with a lid, plus parchment paper.

Makes 1 standard loaf

50 g (¼ cup) active starter

325 g (1⅓ cups) water

300 g (2 cups) strong white bread flour

200 g (1½ cups) whole grain spelt flour

7 g (1 tsp) salt, or to taste

100 g (½ cup) raw pumpkin seeds, for crust (see Note)

STEP 1: In the early evening, in a large mixing bowl, mix together all the ingredients, except the seeds, into a shaggy dough. Cover the bowl with a clean shower cap or your choice of cover and leave it to sit for 1 hour.

STEP 2: After an hour or so, perform the first set of pulls and folds on the dough. Cover the bowl again and leave it on the counter.

STEP 3: Over the next few hours, perform 3 more sets of pulls and folds on the dough, covering the dough after each set.

STEP 4: Perform the final set before going to bed. Leave the covered bowl on the counter overnight, typically 8 to 10 hours, at 64 to 68°F (18 to 20°C).

STEP 5: In the morning, you should be greeted by a bowl of full dough, typically at least doubled. Put the pumpkin seeds into another medium to large bowl. Perform one last set of pulls and folds, once around the bowl, to pull the dough into a ball. Place your hand over the whole dough, turn the whole bowl over and let the dough fall into your hand. Gently place the dough, smooth side down, in the bowl of pumpkin seeds and gently roll it around for the seeds to stick to the dough, then place it, seeds side down, in the banneton. Sprinkle more seeds down the sides and in a layer across the top of the dough.

(Continued)

Cover the banneton with the same shower cap and place it in the fridge for at least 3 hours; the moisture from the dough will help adhere the seeds to the dough.

STEP 6: After 3 to 10 hours in the fridge, when you are ready to bake, preheat the oven to 425°F (220°C) convection, 450°F (230°C) conventional. For how to bake from a cold start, see page 30.

Remove the cover from the banneton, then place the parchment paper over the top of the banneton and place the pan upside down over the top of them both. With one hand under the banneton and one on the pan, turn it all over together to turn the dough out of the banneton and into the pan.

With your bread lame, score an X in the dough between the seeds, put the lid on the pan and bake for 50 minutes. If you would like more color on your loaf, place the pan back in the hot oven, minus the lid, for 5 to 10 minutes.

STEP 7: Once baked, carefully remove the loaf from the pan, saving the parchment paper for next time, and allow the baked loaf to cool on a wire rack for at least an hour before slicing. Some of the seeds may fall off as you slice, but the majority will stay on. The ones that fall off are great to eat—an extra gift from this wonderfully rustic loaf!

Note:

Always add raw seeds to the outside of doughs, as the seeds roast while the dough is being baked. If you start with pre-roasted seeds they will burn.

Top Tip:

Try replacing the pumpkin seeds with sunflower seeds.

The Emmer and Seeds Master

Emmer is one of the most ancient grains that bread was ever made from. It is so tasty and a terrific addition to any loaf. Being an ancient grain, emmer is a weaker flour than bread flour and therefore benefits from being used with slightly less water. The addition of the seeds to the dough will make it quite stiff initially, but it will soften and stretch as you work with it and you will be left with a wonderfully firm dough. It might be slightly sticky to work with, but the result will be a glorious seed-studded loaf full of flavor and goodness.

I like to add roasted seeds to doughs; see page 182 for how to roast.

PREP: Feed all of your starter at room temperature 30 grams (¼ cup) of flour and 30 grams (⅛ cup) of water. Once it is active and ready to use, begin your dough. Prepare a round banneton or bowl with rice flour (see page 14) and set aside a large baking pan with a lid, plus parchment paper.

Makes 1 standard loaf

50 g (¼ cup) active starter

325 g (1⅓ cups) water

300 g (2½ cups) strong white bread flour

200 g (1¾ cups) emmer flour

50 g (½ cup) seeds, either a mix of pumpkin seeds, sunflower seeds and flaxseeds, or any single amount of one type

7 g (1 tsp) salt, or to taste

STEP 1: In the evening, in a large mixing bowl, roughly mix together all the ingredients. Cover the bowl with a clean shower cap or your choice of cover and leave it to sit for 2 hours.

STEP 2: After 2 hours, do the first set of pulls and folds until the dough comes together into a ball. This dough might be a bit stiff, and a bit sticky, but it will give as you work with it. Cover the bowl again and leave it on the counter for an hour or so.

STEP 3: Over the next few hours, perform 3 more sets of pulls and folds on the dough; each time, the dough will become easier to lift and stretch and will require fewer and fewer actions to pull it into a ball. Each time the dough has come together into a ball, cover the bowl again.

STEP 4: Perform the final set of pulls and folds before going to bed. Cover the bowl and leave it on the counter overnight, typically 8 to 10 hours, at 64 to 68°F (18 to 20°C).

STEP 5: In the morning, the dough will have grown with an almost smooth surface and lots of texture underneath. With a final set of pulls and folds, pull the dough into a firm ball.

Sprinkle more rice flour into your banneton and gently place the dough, smooth side down, in the banneton, then sprinkle extra rice flour down the sides and across the top of the dough.

Cover the banneton with the same shower cap and place it in the fridge for at least 3 hours.

STEP 6: After a minimum of 3 hours and before a maximum of 10 hours in the fridge, when you are ready to bake, preheat the oven to 425°F (220°C) convection or 450°F (230°C) conventional. For how to bake from a cold start, see page 30.

Remove the cover from the banneton, then place the parchment paper over the banneton and the pan upside down over the top of them both. With one hand under the banneton and one on the pan, turn it all over together to turn the dough out of the banneton and into the pan.

The dough will be wonderfully firm and a joy to score. I scored mine with my favorite star. Put the lid on the pan and bake for 50 minutes. After 50 minutes, if you would like more color on your loaf, place the pan back in the hot oven, minus the lid, for 5 to 10 minutes.

STEP 7: Once baked, carefully remove the loaf from the pan, saving the parchment paper for next time, and allow the baked loaf to cool on a wire rack for at least an hour before slicing.

The Oat-Crusted Einkorn Master

Einkorn is the oldest of the ancient grains. It is a fine soft flour, so in this recipe I have reduced the amount of water to allow for its softness. Adding an oat crust to the loaf adds to the flavor, but feel free to make this loaf minus the oat crust, if you wish.

PREP: Feed all of your starter 30 grams (¼ cup) of flour and 30 grams (⅛ cup) of water. Once it is active and ready to use, begin your dough. Prepare a round banneton or bowl with rice flour (see page 14) and set aside a large baking pan with a lid, plus parchment paper.

Makes 1 standard loaf

50 g (¼ cup) active starter

300 g (scant 1¼ cups) water

300 g (2½ cups) strong white bread flour

200 g (2 cups) whole grain einkorn flour

7 g (1 tsp) salt, or to taste

50 g (¼ cup) raw oats, for crust (thick-cut/steel-cut oats work perfectly)

STEP 1: In the early evening, in a large mixing bowl, roughly mix together all the ingredients, except the oats. Cover the bowl with your choice of cover and leave it on the counter for 1 hour.

STEP 2: After about an hour, perform the first set of pulls and folds, then cover the bowl again and leave it on the counter for at least an hour.

STEP 3: Perform 3 more sets of pulls and folds over the next few hours. Perform the final set before going to bed. Leave the bowl on the counter overnight, typically 8 to 10 hours, at 64 to 69°F (18 to 20°C).

STEP 4: In the morning, you should be greeted by a bowl full of grown dough. Put the oats into another medium- to large-size bowl. Perform one last set of pulls and folds to form the dough into a nice ball. Place your hand over the whole dough, turn the whole bowl over, and let the dough fall into your hand. Place the dough gently into the bowl of oats and carefully roll it around. Place the oat-covered dough in the banneton oat side down. Sprinkle more oats down the sides and across the top. Cover the banneton and place it in the fridge for 3 to 10 hours.

STEP 5: When you are ready to bake, preheat the oven to 425°F (220°C) convection or 450°F (230°C) conventional. For how to bake from a cold start, see page 30. Remove the cover from the banneton, then place the parchment paper over the banneton and the pan upside down over the top of them both. With one hand under the banneton and one on the pan, turn it all over together to turn the dough into the pan. Score the dough. Put the lid on and bake for 50 minutes. After 50 minutes, if you would like more color on your loaf, place the pan back in the hot oven, minus the lid, for 5 to 10 minutes.

STEP 6: Once baked, carefully remove the loaf from the pan and allow the baked loaf to cool on a wire rack for at least an hour before slicing.

The White and Emmer Grains Master

Cooked whole grains are a wonderful addition to sourdough. The dough loves them and they add a wonderful texture and flavor, as well as their whole grain goodness, to the baked loaf.

You may find emmer grains under the name "farro"; alternatively, you could use cooked spelt grains in this loaf. I have paired the grains with a white loaf, using my master recipe process, for you to be able to really taste and enjoy the added grains.

PREP: Feed all of your starter 30 grams (¼ cup) of flour and 30 grams (⅛ cup) of water. Once it is ready to use, begin your dough. Prepare a round banneton or bowl with rice flour (see page 14) and set aside a large baking pan with a lid, plus parchment paper.

Makes 1 standard loaf

50 g (¼ cup) active starter

350 g (scant 1½ cups) water

500 g (4 cups) strong white bread flour

150 g (1 cup) cooked grains (see page 182)

7 g (1 tsp) salt, or to taste

STEP 1: In the early evening, in a large mixing bowl, roughly mix together all the ingredients, including the grains, until you have a shaggy rough dough. Cover the bowl with a clean shower cap or your choice of cover and leave the bowl on the counter for 1 hour.

STEP 2: After an hour or so, perform the first set of pulls and folds until the dough feels less sticky and comes together into a soft ball. You will be able to feel the grains, but it will be easy to stretch the dough. Cover the bowl again and leave it on your counter.

STEP 3: Over the next few hours, do 3 more sets of pulls and folds on the dough, covering the dough after each set. Perform the final set before going to bed.

STEP 4: Leave the covered bowl on the counter overnight, typically 8 to 10 hours, at 64 to 68°F (18 to 20°C).

STEP 5: In the morning, you will notice how grown and happy the dough is with the added boost of the grains; it may well have grown even more than your dough usually does without the addition of grains.

Gently but firmly perform a final set of pulls and folds on the dough to pull it into a ball. The dough will be bouncy and have a satisfying resistance you will be able to feel.

Place the dough, smooth side down, in the banneton, cover with the same shower cap and place in the fridge for at least 3 hours.

STEP 6: After 3 to 10 hours, when you are ready to bake, preheat the oven to 425°F (220°C) convection or 450°F (230°C) conventional. For how to bake from a cold start, see page 30.

Remove the cover from the banneton, then place the parchment paper over the top of the banneton and the pan upside down over the top of them both. With one hand under the banneton and one on the pan, turn it all over together to turn the dough out of the banneton and into the pan.

Score the dome of the dough; I scored my loaf with a 5-point star. Put the lid on and bake for 50 minutes. After 50 minutes, if you would like more color on your loaf, place the pan back in the hot oven, minus the lid, for 5 to 10 minutes.

STEP 7: Once baked, carefully remove the loaf from the pan, saving the parchment paper for next time, and allow the baked loaf to cool on a wire rack for at least an hour before slicing.

Top Tip:
Try replacing the emmer grains with cooked spelt or einkorn grains (see page 182 for how to cook).

The Whole Wheat and Quinoa Master

I love quinoa, so it was an obvious marriage to add some to my sourdough. And sourdough adores cooked quinoa. It is also a great source of protein, which the dough really responds to.

PREP: Feed your starter 30 grams (¼ cup) of flour and 30 grams (⅛ cup) of water. Once it is active and ready to use, begin your dough. Prepare a round banneton or bowl with rice flour (see page 14) and set aside a large baking pan with a lid, plus parchment paper.

Makes 1 standard loaf

50 g (¼ cup) active starter

350 g (scant 1½ cups) water

400 g (3¼ cups) strong white bread flour

100 g (¾ cup) whole wheat flour

150 g (1 cup) cooked white quinoa (see Top Tips and page 182)

7 g (1 tsp) salt, or to taste

Top Tips:

Optionally, use a red and/or black quinoa mix for added color fun.

Try adding cooked freekeh or siyez to your next dough.

STEP 1: In the early evening, in a large mixing bowl, roughly mix together all the ingredients, including the quinoa. Cover the bowl with your choice of cover and leave it on the counter for 1 hour.

STEP 2: After an hour, perform the first set of pulls and folds. Cover the bowl and leave it on your counter.

STEP 3: Over the next few hours, perform 3 more sets of pulls and folds on the dough, covering the dough after each set. Perform the final set before going to bed. Leave the covered bowl on the counter overnight, typically 8 to 10 hours, at 64 to 68°F (18 to 20°C).

STEP 4: In the morning, gently perform a last set of pulls and folds on the dough to bring it into a nice ball. Carefully lift the dough from the bowl and place it gently into your prepared banneton. Sprinkle more rice flour across the top and down the sides of the dough, cover it again and place it in the fridge for at least 3 hours.

STEP 5: After chilling the dough for 3 to 10 hours, when you are ready to bake, preheat the oven to 425°F (220°C) convection or 450°F (230°C) conventional. For how to bake from a cold start, see page 30. Remove the cover from the banneton, then place the parchment paper over the banneton and the pan upside down over the top of them both. With one hand under the banneton and one on the pan, turn it all over together to turn the dough out of the banneton and into the pan.

Score the dough; I scored the loaf in the photo with petals coming outward from the middle of the dough. Put the lid on and bake for 50 minutes. After 50 minutes, if you would like more color on your loaf, place the pan back in the oven, minus the lid, for 5 to 10 minutes.

STEP 6: Once baked, carefully remove the loaf from the pan, saving the parchment paper for next time, and allow the baked loaf to cool on a wire rack for at least an hour before slicing.

The Walnut White Spelt Master

Walnuts not only add wonderful flavor and texture to sourdough, but they also often add purple swirls to the baked loaf from their reaction to the iron in the flour and the acidity of the dough. It results in a great-looking loaf with the added benefit of a slight crunch. I have used white flours in this recipe so that you will be able to see and fully celebrate the walnuts.

PREP: Feed all of your starter 30 grams (¼ cup) of flour and 30 grams (⅛ cup) of water. Once it is active, begin your dough. Prepare a round banneton or bowl with rice flour (see page 14) and set aside a large baking pan with a lid, plus parchment paper.

Makes 1 standard loaf

50 g (¼ cup) active starter

350 g (scant 1½ cups) water

300 g (2½ cups) strong white bread flour

200 g (1¼ cups) white spelt flour

75 g (1 cup) raw walnuts—whole or halves

7 g (1 tsp) salt, or to taste

STEP 1: In the early evening, in a large mixing bowl, roughly mix together all the ingredients, including the nuts. Cover the bowl with a clean shower cap or your choice of cover and leave on the counter for 1 hour.

STEP 2: After an hour or so, perform a set of pulls and folds on the dough. You will be able to feel the nuts in the dough, but it will be a silky dough, easy to stretch and fold. Cover the bowl and leave on the counter.

STEP 3: Over the next few hours, perform 3 more sets of these pulls and folds on the dough, covering the bowl after each set. Perform the final set before going to bed. The dough will be bouncy, elastic, silky and studded with the nut pieces.

STEP 4: Leave the covered bowl on the counter overnight, typically 8 to 10 hours, at 64 to 68°F (18 to 20°C).

STEP 5: In the morning, the dough will have nicely grown to double its size and already displaying a slightly purple-gray tint. It will have a lovely bounce and resistance.

Sprinkle some extra rice flour into and around the inside of the banneton. Do a final set of pulls and folds on the dough to bring it into a nice slightly firm ball. Place your dough, smooth side down, in the banneton, cover it with the same shower cap and place it in the fridge for at least 3 hours.

STEP 6: After a minimum of 3 hours and a maximum of 10 in the fridge, when you are ready to bake, preheat the oven to 425°F (220°C) convection or 450°F (230°C) conventional. For how to bake from a cold start, see page 30.

Remove the cover from the banneton, then place the parchment paper over the top of the banneton and the pan upside down over the top of them both. With one hand under the banneton and one on the pan, turn it all over together to turn the dough out of the banneton and into the pan.

With your bread lame, score the dome of the dough cleanly and firmly between the nut pieces; I scored mine in an X. Put the lid on and bake for 50 minutes. After 50 minutes, if you would like more color on your loaf, place the pan back in the hot oven, minus the lid, for 5 to 10 minutes.

STEP 7: Once baked, carefully remove the loaf from the pan, saving the parchment paper for next time, and allow the baked loaf to cool on a wire rack for at least an hour before slicing.

Top Tip:
Next time, try adding a handful of chopped dried figs to the dough along with the walnuts.

The Peanut Butter Batard Master

This loaf marries peanut butter and whole wheat flour for a full-flavored, nutritious, lovely bake. The peanut butter adds great extra flavor to the loaf, really enhancing the sourness, as well as adding a silkiness to the dough as you work with it.

All the master loaves can be made as a round loaf or an oval, or "batard." I have made this one as an oval to show how simply the recipes can be converted to a different shape. The banneton used for this loaf is 11 inches (28 cm) long and the baking pan is 11¾ inches (30 cm).

PREP: Feed all of your starter 50 grams (½ cup) of flour and 50 grams (¼ cup) of water. When it is active and ready to use, begin your dough. Prepare your banneton or a bowl with rice flour (see page 14) and set aside your lidded baking pan of choice, plus parchment paper.

Makes 1 standard loaf

75 g (⅜ cup) active starter

375 g (1½ cups) water

300 g (2½ cups) strong white bread flour

200 g (1⅔ cups) whole wheat flour

200 g (¾ cup) unsalted peanut butter

7 g (1 tsp) salt, or to taste

STEP 1: In the early evening, in a large mixing bowl, roughly mix together all of the ingredients, including the peanut butter, cover the bowl and leave it on the counter for 2 hours. The peanut butter will not yet be incorporated into the dough, which will occur during the pulls and folds to follow.

STEP 2: After 2 hours, start pulling and folding the dough until it comes together into a nice ball. The dough will be heavy but stretchy, as well as sticky as the peanut butter mixes with the other ingredients and the oils loosen up with the warmth of your hands. Cover the bowl and leave it on the counter.

STEP 3: Over the next few hours, do 3 more sets of pulls and folds on the dough, covering the bowl after each set. The peanut butter will continue to mix in and you will be able to feel and see the difference in the dough compared to other doughs that do not include peanut butter. Perform the final set of pulls and folds before going to bed.

STEP 4: Leave the covered bowl on the counter overnight, typically 8 to 10 hours, at 64 to 68°F (18 to 20°C).

STEP 5: In the morning, you will see that the dough loves peanut butter! The dough will have doubled, if not more, overnight, with a smooth surface.

(Continued)

Sprinkle an extra layer of rice flour into the banneton. To place the dough into an oval banneton, lift and pull the dough over itself along one side of the bowl. Turn the bowl around completely to the other side and pull the dough on that side again in a line to create a fat sausage of dough. This will be a firm dough full of strength, but even so, do not be heavy handed; protect the lovely work your starter has done. Gently place the dough, smooth side down, into the banneton, sprinkling extra rice flour down the sides and across the top of the dough, cover it again with the same shower cap and place it in the fridge for at least 3 hours.

For a round banneton, perform a final set of pulls and folds, typically once around the bowl, to pull the dough into a firm ball, then proceed as in the previous step.

STEP 6: After a minimum of 3 hours and a maximum of 10 in the fridge, when you are ready to bake, preheat the oven to 425°F (220°C) convection or 450°F (230°C) conventional. For how to bake from a cold start, see page 30.

Remove the cover from the banneton, then place the parchment paper over the top of the banneton and the pan upside down over the top of them both. With one hand under the banneton and one on the pan, turn it all over together to turn the dough out of the banneton and into the pan.

Score the dough cleanly and decisively; it will be firm and inviting to score. I scored my loaf with a single long line off center, about ⅜ inch (1 cm) deep, along one side.

Put the lid on the pan and bake for 50 minutes. After 50 minutes if you would like more color on your loaf, place the pan back in the hot oven, minus the lid, for 5 to 10 minutes.

STEP 7: Once baked, carefully remove the loaf from the pan, saving the parchment paper for next time, and allow the baked loaf to cool on a wire rack for at least an hour before slicing.

Tip:
Visit page 52 to see step-by-step photos of how to pull the dough together for an oval banneton.

Top Tip:
Try adding 100 grams (about ⅓ cup) of almond butter or 50 grams (3 tablespoons) of cashew butter instead of peanut butter, to experience the different flavors and outcomes.

The All-Purpose Einkorn Master

All-purpose einkorn flour is a soft, pale yellow flour. The bran and wheat germ are removed from the whole grain flour to create this lighter version. Einkorn is a pleasure to work with, but as with all ancient grain flours, it benefits from being supported by a strong flour. Therefore, this loaf is made with strong white bread flour and all-purpose einkorn flour. The dough is enjoyable to work with and the baked loaf tastes wonderful, with a perfect chewiness.

PREP: Feed your starter with 30 grams (¼ cup) of flour and 30 grams (⅛ cup) of water. Once it is active and bubbly and ready to use, begin your dough. Prepare a round banneton or bowl with rice flour (see page 14) and set aside a large baking pan with a lid, plus parchment paper.

Makes 1 standard loaf

50 g (¼ cup) active starter

350 g (scant 1½ cups) water

250 g (2 cups) strong white bread flour

250 g (2 cups) all-purpose einkorn flour

7 g (1 tsp) salt, or to taste

STEP 1: In the early evening, in a large mixing bowl, roughly mix together all the ingredients, leaving the dough shaggy. Cover the bowl and leave it on the counter for 1 hour.

STEP 2: After an hour or so, start the first set of pulls and folds. The dough may be a little sticky, but also stretchy. Once it comes together into a ball, cover the bowl with a clean shower cap or your choice of cover and leave it on the counter.

STEP 3: Over the next few hours, perform 3 more sets of pulls and folds on the dough, covering the bowl after each set. The dough will be nice to work with; it will be nicely stretchy, maybe a little spongy, and will come together into a nice soft ball each time. Finish the process by completing a single round of pulls and folds in the bowl, bringing the dough back together into a ball, before going to bed.

STEP 4: Leave the covered bowl on the counter overnight, typically 8 to 10 hours, at 64 to 68°F (18 to 20°C).

STEP 5: In the morning, the dough will have grown, possibly even more than double its original size, with a smooth surface, perhaps blowing a few bubbles. Sprinkle some extra rice flour around the inside of the banneton. Using the same pulling and folding action, pull the dough into a nice firm ball without crushing it. If the dough seems to collapse, it will grow back. Place the ball of dough, rounded side down, in your banneton, cover it again with the same shower cap and place it in the fridge for at least 3 hours.

(Continued)

STEP 6: After 3 to 10 hours in the fridge, when you are ready to bake, preheat the oven to 425°F (200°C) convection or 450°F (230°C) conventional. For how to bake from a cold start, see page 30.

Remove the cover from the banneton, then place the parchment paper over the top of the banneton and the pan upside down over the top of them both. With one hand under the banneton and one on the pan, turn it all over together to turn the dough out of the banneton and into the pan.

Score the dome of dough cleanly and firmly. I scored mine with a 5-point star. Place the lid on the pan, and bake for 50 minutes. After 50 minutes, if you would like more color on your loaf, place the pan back in the hot oven, minus the lid, for 5 to 10 minutes.

STEP 7: Once baked, carefully remove the loaf from the pan, saving the parchment paper for next time if it is not too crisp, and allow the baked loaf to cool on a wire rack for at least an hour before slicing.

BABY MASTER
Sourdough Boules

These smaller-sized loaves are perfect if the standard master recipe loaves are too big for your household, or you just fancy making some cute, smaller loaves. They are also a great size for experimenting with new flours and mixes, as they are made with a total of 300 grams (10.5 ounces) of flour in the dough.

The scaled-down amounts represent two-thirds of those in a standard-sized dough, with some variations in the water quantity depending on the flours used.

I use smaller-sized bannetons for these loaves: round ones measuring 6¾ inches (17 cm) in diameter and 3¼ inches (8.5 cm) deep or oval ones 8¾ inches (22 cm) long, but if you do not have access to one of these, use a bowl of a similar size lined with a clean tea towel and generously drenched with rice flour. Avoid using a regular-sized banneton for these recipes, as the dough will not form the proper shape.

The dough can be baked in the same size pan as for the larger loaves; alternatively, I often use an 8-inch (20-cm)-diameter pan with a lid. If you have a larger oval pan, you could also bake two of these smaller loaves in it at one time.

The baking time is five to ten minutes shorter than for a larger loaf.

If you like these recipes, they can easily be scaled up to make bigger loaves.

Khorasan and Golden Flaxseeds
Baby Master

Khorasan adds a nutty flavor to any loaf. If used alone, this flour would create a dense loaf, so it is ideal paired with a lighter flour, as it is here. This creates a smooth, tactile dough to work with and a lovely tasty loaf.

PREP: Feed all of your starter with 30 grams (¼ cup) of flour and 30 grams (⅛ cup) of water. Once active and bubbly, it is ready to use; now begin your dough. Prepare a mini banneton or small mixing bowl with rice flour (see page 14) and set aside a baking pan with a lid, plus parchment paper.

Makes 1 small loaf

50 g (¼ cup) active starter

225 g (scant 1 cup) water

200 g (1¾ cups) strong white bread flour

100 g (¾ cup) whole grain Khorasan flour

40 g (¼ cup) golden flaxseeds

4 g (½ tsp) salt, or to taste

STEP 1: In the early evening, in a large mixing bowl, roughly mix together all the ingredients and cover the bowl with a clean shower cap or your choice of cover. Leave it on the counter for 1 hour. The dough may be quite firm at this point.

STEP 2: After an hour, perform the first set of pulls and folds on the dough. The dough will be soft and stretchy. Once the dough comes together into a soft ball, cover and leave on the counter.

STEP 3: Over the next few hours, perform 3 more sets of pulls and folds on the dough, covering the bowl after each set. The dough will become soft and stretchy and will come together into a ball with very few actions. Perform the last set before going to bed.

STEP 4: Leave the covered bowl on the counter overnight, typically 8 to 10 hours, at 64 to 68°F (18 to 20°C).

STEP 5: In the morning, the dough should have doubled, if not nearly tripled, with a smooth surface. Gently perform a final set of pulls and folds, once around the bowl, to pull the dough into a ball. The dough will be soft, but will come together into a nice ball. Place the dough in the banneton. Sprinkle extra rice flour across the top of the dough and down the sides of the banneton. Cover with the same shower cap and place in the fridge for at least 3 hours.

STEP 6: After 3 to 10 hours in the fridge, when you are ready to bake, preheat the oven to 425°F (220°C) convection or 450°F (230°C) conventional. For how to bake from a cold start, see page 30.

Remove the cover from the banneton, then place the parchment paper over the top of the banneton and the pan upside down over the top of them both. With one hand under the banneton and one on the pan, turn it all over together to turn the dough out of the banneton and into the pan.

With a bread lame or razor blade, score the dome of dough cleanly. I scored my loaf with a 5-point star from the outside inward. Put the lid on the pot and bake for 45 minutes. After 45 minutes, if you would like more color on your loaf, place the pan back in the hot oven, minus the lid, for 5 minutes.

STEP 7: Carefully remove the baked loaf from the hot pan and allow the baked loaf to cool for at least an hour before slicing it.

Einkorn and Grains Baby Master

Einkorn is such a truly wonderful grain; it is the oldest known grain that bread was made from. The actual grains are chewy and full of flavor and goodness. This loaf has both the flour and cooked grains in it, to really celebrate the grain. Einkorn grains generate a lovely fluffy interior in the baked loaf; it is a Boddy household favorite.

PREP: Feed all of your starter 30 grams (¼ cup) of flour and 30 grams (⅛ cup) of water. Once your starter is bubbly and active, begin your dough. Prepare a mini banneton or small mixing bowl with rice flour (see page 14) and set aside a baking pan with a lid, plus parchment paper.

Makes 1 small loaf

30 g (⅛ cup) active starter

200 g (¾ cup plus 1½ tbsp) water

200 g (1⅔ cups) strong white bread flour

100 g (1 cup) whole grain einkorn flour

75 g (¾ cup) cooked einkorn grains (see page 182)

4 g (½ tsp) salt, or to taste

STEP 1: In the evening, in a large mixing bowl, roughly mix together all the ingredients, including the grains. Cover the bowl with a clean shower cap or your choice of cover and leave on the counter for 1 hour.

STEP 2: After an hour or so, perform the first set of pulls and folds. The dough may start off being quite sticky, if you find it too sticky, use a curved dough scraper to work with the dough on this occasion, it will become less sticky, the more you work with it. Cover the bowl and leave it on the counter.

STEP 3: Over the next few hours, perform 3 more sets of pulls and folds on the dough, covering the bowl after each set. It will become softer and stretchier and less sticky with each handling. Perform the last set before going to bed, bringing the dough into a ball.

STEP 4: Leave the covered bowl on the counter overnight, typically 8 to 10 hours, at 64 to 68°F (18 to 20°C).

STEP 5: In the morning, the dough should have at least doubled. Perform a final set of pulls and folds to pull the dough into a ball. It may seem to collapse but that is normal. Place the dough, smooth side down, in the banneton. Sprinkle extra rice flour across the top of the dough and down the sides of the banneton. Cover the banneton with the same shower cap and place it in the fridge for at least 3 hours.

STEP 6: After 3 to 10 hours in the fridge, when you are ready to bake, preheat the oven to 425°F (220°C) convection or 450°F (230°C) conventional. For how to bake from a cold start, see page 30.

Remove the cover from the banneton, then place the parchment paper over the top of the banneton and the pan upside down over the top of them both. With one hand under the banneton and one on the pan, turn it all over together to turn the dough out of the banneton and into the pan.

With a bread lame or razor blade, score the dome of the dough. I scored my loaf with 3 strokes meeting in the middle. Put the lid on the pot and bake for 45 minutes. After 45 minutes, if you would like more color on your loaf, place the pan back in the hot oven, minus the lid, for 5 minutes.

STEP 7: Once baked, carefully remove the loaf from the pan, saving the parchment paper for next time, and allow the loaf to cool on a wire rack for at least an hour before slicing.

Flaxseeds and White Spelt Baby Master

White spelt flour is silky, fine and soft. Making a loaf from this flour alone can be a challenge. The flaxseeds in this loaf add flavor and texture, but more importantly, they add support. This loaf has a crisp crust and a wonderful, perfectly chewy interior.

PREP: Feed all of your starter 30 grams (¼ cup) of flour and 30 grams (⅛ cup) of water. Once it is active and bubbly, begin your dough. Prepare a mini banneton with rice flour (see page 14) and set aside a baking pan with a lid, plus parchment paper.

Makes 1 small loaf

30 g (⅛ cup) active starter

200 g (¾ cup plus 1½ tbsp) water

300 g (2⅔ cups) white spelt flour

25 g (⅛ cup) flaxseeds

4 g (½ tsp) salt, or to taste

STEP 1: In the evening, in a large mixing bowl, roughly mix together all the ingredients, including the flaxseeds. Cover the bowl with a clean shower cap or your choice of cover. Leave it on the counter for 1 hour.

STEP 2: After an hour or so, perform the first set of pulls and folds. Cover the bowl again and leave it on the counter.

STEP 3: Over the next few hours, perform 3 more sets of pulls and folds on the dough. Perform the last set before going to bed. Leave the covered bowl on the counter overnight, typically 8 to 10 hours, at 64 to 68°F (18 to 20°C).

STEP 4: In the morning, your dough should have doubled in size. Perform a final set of pulls and folds, to pull the dough into a nice ball. Place the dough, smooth side down, in the banneton. Sprinkle extra rice flour across the top of the dough and down the sides of the banneton. Cover the bowl and place it in the fridge for at least 3 hours.

STEP 5: After 3 to 10 hours in the fridge, when you are ready to bake, preheat the oven to 425°F (220°C) convection or 450°F (230°C) conventional. For how to bake from a cold start, see page 30.

Remove the cover from the banneton, then place the parchment paper over the top of the uncovered banneton and the pan upside down over the top of them both. With one hand under the banneton and one on the pan, turn it all over together to turn out the dough into the pan.

Score the dough. Put the lid on the pot and bake for 45 minutes. After 45 minutes, if you would like more color on your loaf, place the pan back in the hot oven, minus the lid, for 5 minutes.

STEP 6: Once baked, carefully remove the loaf from the pan, saving the parchment paper for next time, and allow the baked loaf to cool on a wire rack for at least an hour before slicing.

Roasted Cashew Baby Master

I love roasted cashews. My challenge with making this dough is not to eat all of the nuts beforehand! They soften while baking but add great flavor and texture and look nice when you slice into the loaf. I used half strong white bread flour and half whole wheat flour in this recipe to celebrate the cashews.

PREP: Feed all of your starter 30 grams (¼ cup) of flour and 30 grams (⅛ cup) of water. Allow it several hours to become active and ready to use. Prepare a mini banneton or small mixing bowl with rice flour (see page 14) and set aside a baking pan with a lid, plus parchment paper.

Makes 1 small loaf

50 g (¼ cup) active starter

225 g (scant 1 cup) water

150 g (1¼ cups) strong white bread flour

150 g (1¼ cups) whole wheat flour

75 g (¾ cup) roasted plain cashews (see page 182)

4 g (½ tsp) salt, or to taste

STEP 1: In the early evening, in a large mixing bowl roughly mix together all the ingredients, including the nuts. Cover the bowl with a clean shower cap or your choice of cover. Leave it on the counter for 1 hour.

STEP 2: After an hour or so, perform the first set of pulls and folds. The dough may start off being quite sticky, but it will become less so the more you work with it. The nuts add a chunkiness to the dough, but it will still be possible to stretch it. Cover the bowl again and leave it on the counter.

STEP 3: Over the next few hours, perform 3 more sets of pulls and folds on the dough, each time pulling it into a ball, covering the bowl after each set. The dough will be silky and stretchy between the nuts. Perform the last set before going to bed.

STEP 4: Leave the covered bowl on the counter overnight, typically 8 to 10 hours, at 64 to 68°F (18 to 20°C).

STEP 5: In the morning, your dough will have grown to at least double in size. Do a final set of pulls and folds, once around the bowl, to pull the dough into a firm ball without crushing or overhandling it. Place the dough, smooth side down, in the banneton. Sprinkle extra rice flour across the top of the dough and down the sides of the banneton if you feel it needs it. Cover the banneton with the same shower cap and place it in the fridge for at least 3 hours.

STEP 6: After 3 to 10 hours in the fridge, when you are ready to bake, preheat the oven to 425°F (220°C) convection or 450°F (230°C) conventional. For how to bake from a cold start, see page 30.

Remove the cover from the banneton, then place the parchment paper over the top of the banneton and the pan upside down over the top of them both. With one hand under the banneton and one on the pan, turn it all over together to turn the dough out of the banneton and into the pan.

With a sharp bread lame, score the dome of the dough firmly between the nuts. I scored mine with an X, cutting from the outer edge inward. Put the lid on the pan and bake for 45 minutes. After 45 minutes, if you would like more color on your loaf, place the pan back in the hot oven, minus the lid, for 5 minutes.

STEP 7: Once baked, carefully remove the loaf from the pan, saving the parchment paper for next time, and allow the loaf to cool on a wire rack for at least an hour before slicing.

Almond, Raisin and Spelt Baby Master

Almond flour adds a wonderful softness and slight sweetness to a loaf, as well as nutrition and protein from the nuts. The honey and raisins give the loaf almost a tea bread–like flavor. This soft loaf has a close crumb and is lovely eaten with cheese and/or jam.

PREP: Feed all of your starter 30 grams (¼ cup) of flour and 30 grams (⅛ cup) of water. Once it is bubbly and active, it is ready to use in your dough. Prepare a mini banneton or small mixing bowl with rice flour (see page 14) and set aside a baking pan with a lid, plus parchment paper.

Makes 1 small loaf

30 g (⅛ cup) active starter

200 g (¾ cup plus 1½ tbsp) water

300 g (2½ cups) white spelt flour

50 g (½ cup) almond flour or ground almonds

50 g (½ cup) raisins

20 g (2 tbsp) runny honey

4 g (½ tsp) salt, or to taste

STEP 1: In the early evening, in a large mixing bowl, roughly mix together all the ingredients. Leave the dough shaggy and cover the bowl with a clean shower cap or cover of your choice. Leave it on the counter for 1 hour.

STEP 2: After an hour or so, perform the first set of pulls and folds on the dough. You will be able to smell the almond flour as you lift the dough. It may start off being quite sticky, but it will become less so the more you work with it. Cover the bowl and leave it on the counter.

STEP 3: Over the next few hours, perform 3 more sets of pulls and folds. The dough will be soft and wonderfully stretchy. During each set, once the dough comes into a ball, cover the bowl again and allow it to sit until next time. Perform the last set before going to bed.

STEP 4: Leave the covered bowl on the counter overnight, typically 8 to 10 hours, at 64 to 68°F (18 to 20°C).

STEP 5: In the morning, the dough will have grown at least double in size. Gently perform a final set of pulls and folds, once around the bowl, to pull the dough into a ball of sorts. It will seem to collapse as you handle it, but will grow back as it develops in the banneton. Gently lift the dough from the bowl and place it, smooth side down, in the banneton. Cover the banneton with the same shower cap and place it in the fridge for at least 3 hours.

STEP 6: After 3 to 10 hours in the fridge, when you are ready to bake, preheat the oven to 425°F (220°C) convection or 450°F (230°C) conventional. For how to bake from a cold start, see page 30.

Remove the cover from the banneton, then place the parchment paper over the top of the banneton and the pan upside down over the top of them both. With one hand under the banneton and one on the pan, turn it all over together to turn the dough out of the banneton and into the pan.

With a bread lame or razor blade, score the dome of the dough. I scored mine with a 5-point star. Put the lid on the pot and bake for 45 minutes. After 45 minutes, if you would like more color on your loaf, place the pan back in the hot oven, minus the lid, for 5 minutes.

STEP 7: Once baked, carefully remove the loaf from the pan, saving the parchment paper for next time, and place it on a wire rack. Allow the baked loaf to cool for at least an hour before slicing.

Einkorn Chia Seed Baby Master

The chia seeds in this dough not only create an attractive loaf, but also support the soft einkorn flour. The dough is sticky and not very easy to shape, but it bakes into a lovely dome with an even spread of the chia seeds throughout. And it tastes great!

PREP: Feed all of your starter 30 grams (¼ cup) of flour and 30 grams (⅛ cup) of water. Once it is active and bubbly, begin your dough. Prepare a mini banneton or small mixing bowl with rice flour (see page 14) and set aside a baking pan with a lid, plus parchment paper.

Makes 1 small loaf

30 g (⅛ cup) active starter

200 g (¾ cup plus 1½ tbsp) water

300 g (2¾ cups) all-purpose einkorn flour

25 g (¼ cup) black chia seeds

4 g (½ tsp) salt, or to taste

STEP 1: In the early evening, in a large mixing bowl, roughly mix together all the ingredients, including the chia seeds, then cover the bowl with your choice of cover. Leave it on the counter for 1 hour.

STEP 2: Perform the first set of pulls and folds until the dough forms a soft ball. Cover the bowl and leave it on the counter.

STEP 3: Over the next few hours, perform 3 more sets of pulls and folds, covering the bowl after each set. Perform the last set before going to bed. Leave the covered bowl on the counter overnight, typically 8 to 10 hours, at 64 to 68°F (18 to 20°C).

STEP 4: In the morning, the dough will have doubled, with a smooth seed-studded surface. Gently perform a final set of pulls and folds, to pull the dough into a ball, then place the dough in the banneton. Sprinkle rice flour across the top of the dough and down the sides. Cover the bowl and place it in the fridge for at least 3 hours.

STEP 5: After 3 to 10 hours in the fridge, when you are ready to bake, preheat the oven to 425°F (220°C) convection or 450°F (230°C) conventional. For how to bake from a cold start, see page 30.

Remove the cover from the banneton, then place the parchment paper over the top of the banneton and the pan base upside down over the top of them both. With one hand under the banneton and one on the pan, turn it all over together to turn the dough out of the banneton and into the pan.

Score the dough. I scored mine with a Y. Put the lid on the pot and bake for 40 minutes. After 40 minutes, if you would like more color on your loaf, place the pan back in the hot oven, minus the lid, for 5 more minutes.

STEP 6: Once baked, carefully remove the loaf from the pan, saving the parchment paper for next time, and allow the baked loaf to cool on a wire rack for at least an hour before slicing.

MASTER
Sourdough Focaccia

Sourdough focaccia is a holey, airy bread with a perfectly crunchy base. This focaccia is made using my master recipe dough. In the recipes that follow, I use smaller quantities, though the focaccia can also be made using the standard full-sized dough (page 27). The method follows the same step-by-step process, from the first rough mixing of the dough to allowing it to proof overnight. At this point, the process is amended to create the focaccia.

These recipes are best started the evening before you expect to serve the baked focaccia.

Focaccia is wonderful fresh from the oven and just as wonderful several hours later, or warmed up again the next day. Reheat by preheating the oven to 400°F (200°C) convection or 425°F (220°C) conventional, placing the bread on a baking sheet and warming for 5 to 10 minutes to make the base crunchy again.

Note that the various recipes work better with differently sized pans as I have stated in the recipes—either an 8-inch (20-cm) round or square pan or a medium baking sheet, about 10 x 14 inches (26 x 36 cm).

Top Tips:

At Step 5, if you are not ready to bake your focaccia the next morning, place the bowl of dough in the fridge to stop it from proofing any more at that point. Then, when you are ready to make the focaccia, take the dough from the fridge at least an hour beforehand for it to warm up to room temperature and therefore be easier to handle, then continue with Step 5.

To create a pizza base, follow the same steps but make the dough much thinner and reduce the olive oil coating.

Garlic, Rye and Olive Oil Focaccia

Imagine focaccia with the flavor of sourdough, topped with garlic and olive oil. This recipe will give you all of that as well as the wonderful depth of flavor from the rye flour, which enhances that of the sourdough.

PREP: Feed all of your starter with 30 grams (¼ cup) of flour and 30 grams (⅛ cup) of water. When it is active and ready, begin your dough.

Makes 1 medium-sized focaccia

50 g (¼ cup) active starter

200 g (¾ cup plus 1½ tbsp) water

250 g (2 cups) strong white bread flour

50 g (½ cup) dark rye flour

3 g (½ tsp) salt, or to taste

Olive oil, for drizzling

4 fat cloves garlic, peeled, each sliced into thirds lengthwise

STEP 1: In the evening, in a large mixing bowl, roughly mix together all the ingredients, except the olive oil and garlic. Cover the bowl with a clean shower cap or your choice of cover and leave it on the counter for 1 hour.

STEP 2: After about an hour, perform the first set of pulls and folds on the dough. This dough may be quite sticky due to the inclusion of rye. Cover the bowl and leave it on the counter.

STEP 3: After another hour, perform 1 more set of pulls and folds on the dough until the dough comes together into a ball. Leave the covered bowl on the counter overnight, 8 to 10 hours, at 64 to 68°F (18 to 20°C).

STEP 4: The next morning, the dough should have doubled and possibly even tripled, and is now ready to be used to make focaccia. Prepare a medium baking sheet by liberally drizzling it with a good amount of olive oil. I aim for 3 tablespoons (45 ml) of oil. Move the pan around to spread the oil all over the surface.

Using a bowl scraper or your hands, gently ease the bubbly risen dough from the bowl onto the prepared pan. Gently turn the dough over once to cover it completely with the oil. Cover the entire pan loosely with a large plastic bag or plastic wrap and leave it on the counter for 1½ to 2 hours.

STEP 5: To bake, preheat the oven to 400°F (200°C) convection or 425°F (220°C) conventional. Using your fingertips, push the dough into a rectangular or oval shape until it is about 1 inch (2 to 3 cm) thick. Use your fingertips to firmly press dimples all over the dough. Sprinkle the garlic evenly over the dough, then bake for 18 to 20 minutes, or until browned.

STEP 6: Remove the baked focaccia from the oven and let it rest in the pan for 20 minutes, then ease the baked bread off of the pan, transfer it to a board or large plate, cut it into pieces and serve.

Cooked Spelt Grain–Studded Focaccia

I like any excuse to add cooked grains to my bakes, including focaccia. The proofing dough loves the addition of the whole grains, and the baked bread has a great chewiness from the cooked grains running through it.

PREP: Feed all of your starter with 30 grams (¼ cup) of flour and 30 grams (⅛ cup) of water. Once it is active, begin your dough.

Makes 1 medium-sized focaccia

50 g (¼ cup) active starter

200 g (¾ cup plus 1½ tbsp) water

150 g (1⅔ cups) strong white bread flour

150 g (1½ cups) whole grain spelt flour

75 g (¾ cup) cooked spelt grain (see page 182)

3 g (½ tsp) salt, or to taste

Olive oil, for drizzling

STEP 1: In the early evening, in a large mixing bowl, roughly mix together all the ingredients, except the olive oil. Cover the bowl with a clean shower cap or your choice of cover and leave it on the counter for 2 hours.

STEP 2: After the 2 hours, perform the first set of pulls and folds on the dough until it comes together into a soft ball. Cover the bowl and leave it on the counter.

STEP 3: After another hour, do 1 more set of pulls and folds on the dough until it comes together into a ball. This dough will be soft and stretchy and will easily form a ball. Leave the covered bowl on the counter overnight, typically 8 to 10 hours, at 64 to 68°F (18 to 20°C).

STEP 4: The next morning, the dough will have doubled, if not more. It is now ready to use to make focaccia. Drizzle a good amount of olive oil, 2 to 3 tablespoons (30 to 45 ml), all over an 8-inch (20-cm) round or square baking pan, tipping the pan around to spread the oil.

Using a bowl scraper or your hands, gently ease the bubbly risen dough from the bowl onto the prepared pan. Do this gently and do not handle the dough too much. Gently turn the dough over in the pan to cover it completely with oil. Cover the entire pan loosely with a large plastic bag, or plastic wrap and leave it on the counter for 1½ to 2 hours.

STEP 5: To bake, preheat the oven to 400°F (200°C) convection or 425°F (220°C) conventional. Using your fingertips, push the dough out to fill the pan. Use your fingertips again to firmly press dimples all over the dough. Bake for 18 to 20 minutes, or until browned.

STEP 6: Remove the baked focaccia from the oven and let it rest in the pan for 15 to 20 minutes to cool slightly and loosen, then ease the bread off of the pan with a spatula and serve immediately.

Einkorn and Raisin Focaccia

This baked loaf tastes almost like a tea bread we would eat in England, slathered with butter. For an added sweetness, finish with a flourish of sugar or cinnamon sugar.

PREP: Feed all of your starter with 30 grams (¼ cup) of flour and 30 grams (⅛ cup) of water. When it is active and ready, begin your dough.

Makes 1 medium-sized focaccia

50 g (¼ cup) active starter

100 g (scant ½ cup) water

100 g (scant ½ cup) whole milk or milk of your choice, dairy or nondairy

150 g (1¼ cups) strong white bread flour

150 g (1½ cups) whole grain einkorn flour

50 g (½ cup) raisins (preferably nice, fat raisins)

3 g (½ tsp) salt, or to taste

Olive oil, for drizzling

Top Tip:
If you prefer, replace the raisins with your choice of dried fruit.

STEP 1: In the early evening, in a large mixing bowl, roughly mix together all the ingredients except the olive oil. Cover the bowl with a clean shower cap or your choice of cover and let it sit on the counter for 2 hours.

STEP 2: After 2 hours, do the first set of pulls and folds on the dough to build it up. This dough will start off sticky, but it will be slightly stretchy. Cover the bowl and leave it on the counter.

STEP 3: After an hour or so, perform 1 more set of pulls and folds on the dough. It will remain sticky and may not come together into a firm ball. Leave the covered bowl on the counter overnight, typically 8 to 10 hours, at 64 to 68°F (18 to 20°C).

STEP 4: The next morning, the dough will have at least doubled, and is now ready to use to make focaccia. For a smaller, fuller, thicker focaccia like in the photo, use an 8-inch (20-cm) square or round pan. For a thinner, crunchy focaccia, use a bigger baking sheet. Prepare your choice of baking pan by liberally drizzling it with olive oil, 2 to 3 tablespoons (30 to 45 ml).

Using a bowl scraper or your hands, gently ease the bubbly risen dough from the bowl onto the prepared pan. Be careful not to squash it too much and gently turn it over in the oil so that it is covered completely with olive oil. Cover the pan loosely with plastic wrap and leave it on the counter for 1½ to 2 hours.

STEP 5: Preheat the oven to 400°F (200°C) convection or 425°F (220°C) conventional. Using your fingertips, push the dough out to the corners of the smaller pan. Or in the larger pan, push it into a rectangular or oval shape until it is about 1 inch (2 to 3 cm) thick. Use your fingertips to firmly press dimples all over the dough. Bake for 18 to 20 minutes, or until browned.

STEP 6: Remove the baked focaccia from the oven and let it rest in the pan for 15 to 20 minutes, then ease the baked bread off of the pan, transfer it to a board or large plate, cut it into pieces and serve.

Spelt and Cheese Focaccia

Spelt cheesy fabulousness! The combination of earthy spelt flour with your favorite cheese baked to a light holey bread is glorious. Spelt flour works perfectly in focaccia; it adds a crunchy base, as well as a biscuit-like flavor.

PREP: Feed all of your starter with 30 grams (¼ cup) of flour and 30 grams (⅛ cup) of water. When it is active and ready, begin your dough.

Makes 1 medium-sized focaccia

50 g (¼ cup) active starter

200 g (scant 1 cup) water

150 g (1¼ cups) strong white bread flour

150 g (1½ cups) whole grain spelt flour

150 g (1½ cups) hard cheese (like Cheddar), cut into ¼" (5-mm) cubes

3 g (½ tsp) salt, or to taste

Olive oil, for drizzling

STEP 1: In the early evening, in a large mixing bowl, roughly mix together all the ingredients except the olive oil. Cover the bowl with a clean shower cap or your choice of cover and let it sit on the counter for 2 hours.

STEP 2: After 2 hours, do the first set of pulls and folds. This dough may be stiff; it may be easier to fold into itself than stretch at this point. Cover the bowl and leave it on the counter.

STEP 3: After an hour or so, do 1 more set of pulls and folds. The dough will be easier to stretch and come together into a lumpy ball.

STEP 4: Leave the covered bowl on the counter overnight, 8 to 10 hours, at 64 to 68°F (18 to 20°C).

STEP 5: The next morning, the dough will have doubled and is now ready to be used to make focaccia. Prepare a medium or large baking sheet by liberally drizzling it with a good amount of olive oil, 2 to 3 tablespoons (30 to 45 ml).

Using a bowl scraper or your hands, gently ease the bubbly risen dough from the bowl onto the prepared pan. Be careful not to squash the dough too much and gently turn it over in the oil so that it is covered completely with olive oil. Cover the entire pan loosely with a large plastic bag or plastic wrap and leave it on the counter for 1½ to 2 hours.

STEP 6: Preheat the oven to 400°F (200°C) convection or 425°F (220°C) conventional. Using your fingertips, firmly press dimples all over the dough until it is 1 inch (2 to 3 cm) deep and an oval shape in the middle of the pan. Bake for 18 to 20 minutes, or until browned.

STEP 7: Remove the baked focaccia from the oven and let it rest in the pan for 15 to 20 minutes, then ease the baked bread off of the pan, transfer it to a board or large plate, cut it into pieces and serve.

Whole Wheat, Tomato and Garlic Focaccia

This is another version of my master recipe focaccia. This shows that any mix of flours and toppings can be used; these recipes are just a few of my combinations. Feel free to have fun playing with the recipe!

PREP: Feed all of your starter with 30 grams (¼ cup) of flour and 30 grams (⅛ cup) of water. When it is active and ready, begin your dough.

Makes 1 medium-sized focaccia

50 g (¼ cup) active starter

200 g (¾ cup plus 1½ tbsp) water

150 g (1⅓ cups) white spelt flour

150 g (1⅓ cups) whole wheat flour

12 cherry tomatoes, halved

3 g (½ tsp) salt, or to taste

Optional: caramelized onion and/or roasted garlic

Olive oil, for drizzling

4 fat cloves garlic, peeled, each sliced into thirds lengthwise

STEP 1: In the early evening, in a large mixing bowl, mix together all the ingredients, including the halved tomatoes and caramelized onion or roasted garlic (if using), except the olive oil and fresh garlic. Cover the bowl with a clean shower cap or your choice of cover and leave it on the counter for 2 hours.

STEP 2: After the 2 hours, perform a set of pulls and folds until the dough comes together into a soft ball. This dough will be nicely stretchy while dotted with the tomatoes. Cover the bowl again and leave it on the counter.

STEP 3: After another hour, perform 1 more set of pulls and folds on the dough until it comes together into a ball.

STEP 4: Leave the covered bowl on the counter overnight, typically 8 to 10 hours, at 64 to 68°F (18 to 20°C).

STEP 5: The next morning, the dough will have doubled, and it will be nice and firm. It is now ready to use to make focaccia. If you like a thinner, crunchy focaccia as shown in the photo, use a medium to large baking sheet; if you like a thicker focaccia, use an 8-inch (20-cm) round or square pan.

Prepare your choice of baking pan by liberally drizzling it with a good amount of olive oil, around 3 tablespoons (45 ml), and move the pan around to spread the oil all over it. Using a bowl scraper or your hands, gently ease the bubbly risen dough from the bowl onto the prepared pan. Carefully turn the dough over in the pan to cover it completely with olive oil. Cover the entire pan loosely with a large plastic bag or plastic wrap and leave it on the counter for 1½ to 2 hours.

(Continued)

Whole Wheat, Tomato and Garlic Focaccia (Continued)

STEP 6: To bake, preheat the oven to 400°F (200°C) convection or 425°F (220°C) conventional. Using your fingertips, push the dough out to a rectangular or oval shape until it is about 1 inch (2.5 cm) thick, or to the edges if you are using a smaller pan. Use your fingertips to firmly press dimples all over the dough.

Sprinkle the garlic evenly over the dough, drizzle with a little extra olive oil, then bake for 18 to 20 minutes, or until browned.

STEP 7: Remove the baked focaccia from the oven and let it rest in the pan for 15 to 20 minutes, then ease the baked bread off of the pan, transfer it to a board or large plate, cut it into pieces and serve.

Top Tips:

Enjoy dimpling the dough, it will spring back up during baking.

If you are using a nonstick pan you will be able to remove the baked focaccia from the pan immediately.

The base of the bread will be oily, keep this in mind when you serve and eat it.

Same-Day Sourdough Focaccia Timetable

All the focaccia recipes can be converted to a same-day process by using the following timetable. With this method, the dough will be ready to serve at 6:00 p.m. This is just a guide, and these times can be shifted up or back depending on your needs.

STEP 1: The evening before, feed your starter with 30 grams (¼ cup) of flour and 30 grams (⅛ cup) of water and allow it to become active overnight. Alternatively, first thing in the morning, feed it at room temperature with warm water, then place it in a warm spot, ideally 73 to 75°F (23 to 24°C), to become active.

STEP 2: At 10:00 a.m., in a large mixing bowl, roughly mix together all of the ingredients, cover the bowl with a clean shower cap or your choice of cover and place it in your oven with the light on and door propped open (see page 34).

STEP 3: At 11:00 a.m., perform a single set of pulls and folds, several times around the bowl.

Cover the bowl again and place it back in the oven with the light on and door open, or again in your warm spot.

STEP 4: At 4:00 p.m., remove the dough and flop it onto your olive oil–prepared pan and entirely cover the pan with a large plastic bag or plastic wrap. Leave it on your counter at room temperature.

STEP 5: At 5:00 p.m., dimple and bake the bread.

STEP 6: Remove the baked bread from the oven and let it rest on the hot pan for 15 to 20 minutes to slightly cool and loosen up before serving.

BUTTERMILK
Sourdough Biscuits

These tasty morsels are my sourdough take on biscuits, or what we would call savory buttermilk scones in the U.K. The use of sourdough starter gives them a great texture and flavor and provides another way to use your starter. The inclusion of buttermilk and baking soda makes these biscuits faster to make than a loaf, as there is no waiting time.

These can be made with bubbly active starter or with dormant starter that you have fed and used within the last week, assuming you have enough starter to leave yourself with some. In these recipes, the starter adds its own taste and texture, not rise.

I have several suggestions for using different flours and adding different ingredients and flavors to these beauties. Once you have tried my versions, do feel free to let your imagination go wild!

Top Tips:

These are quick recipes. Once your starter is ready, the dough takes 10 to 15 minutes to mix and cut into rounds and only 16 to 18 minutes to bake.

If you do not have buttermilk, mix 1¼ cups (284 ml) of whole milk with 1½ tablespoons (22.5 ml) of fresh lemon juice or white vinegar. Allow the mixture time to thicken for 5 to 10 minutes before using. Alternatively, use a mixture of half natural or plain yogurt and half water.

These are great warm, especially with their crunchy surface, but they also taste great later once cooled and their flavor has developed. They are best eaten on the day of baking, but any leftovers can be stored in an airtight container. They will soften but can be freshened up by placing them in a preheated oven—350°F (180°C) convection or 400°F (200°C) conventional—for 5 minutes.

White and Wonderful Buttermilk Biscuits

These are my original sourdough buttermilk biscuits. They are light and textured and wonderfully savory. This recipe forms the basis for the three recipes that follow it.

PREP: To generate 85 grams (scant ½ cup) of active starter, feed all of your starter 50 grams (½ cup) of flour and 50 grams (¼ cup) of water several hours before you plan to make the dough.

Makes 15 or 16 biscuits

85 g (scant ½ cup) active starter or unfed starter

350 g (2⅔ cups) all-purpose flour, plus more for dusting

300 g (1¼ cups) buttermilk

7 g (1½ tsp) baking soda

4 g (½ tsp) salt, or to taste

STEP 1: In a mixing bowl, use a strong spatula or your hand to mix together all the ingredients until well combined. This mixture is soft and sticky and does not benefit from being overworked or handled too much. It does not need to be kneaded, just mixed into a nice soft dough.

STEP 2: Preheat the oven to 400°F (200°C) convection or 425°F (220°C) conventional. Line a large baking sheet with parchment paper.

Turn out the dough onto a well-floured counter and spread and push it with your hands to flatten it out to a ¾-inch (2-cm)-thick disk.

Use a 2½-inch (6-cm)-round cookie cutter or a similarly sized glass to cut out the biscuits: Push the cutter directly downward, then remove it directly upward—do not twist it to cut or release the dough—otherwise, you will lose the neat edge and the biscuits will not rise. You may need to use a palette knife or spatula to lift the rounds from the counter.

Place the rounds on the prepared baking sheet. They can be close together, as they do not spread outward. Once you have cut out as many rounds as possible from the dough, bring the rest of the dough together again, push it back down into a disk ¾ inch (2 cm) thick, and cut out more rounds. Keep doing this until you have cut out all of the biscuits.

STEP 3: Bake for 16 to 18 minutes, or until nicely browned.

STEP 4: Remove the biscuits from the oven and transfer them to a wire rack to cool—resist eating immediately and burning your mouth. They will have a crunchy exterior and a soft interior.

Cheesy Spelt Buttermilk Biscuits

What is better than a melty cheesy morsel?! Add to that the flavor of sourdough and the lovely spelt flours, and these biscuits are very moreish.

PREP: To generate 85 grams (scant ½ cup) of active starter, feed all of your starter 50 grams (½ cup) of flour and 50 grams (¼ cup) of water several hours before you plan to make the dough.

Makes 15 or 16 biscuits

85 g (scant ½ cup) active starter or unfed starter

200 g (1¾ cups) white spelt flour, plus more for dusting

150 g (1¼ cups) whole grain spelt flour

75 g (½ cup) grated mature Cheddar cheese (or your choice of another strongly flavored cheese)

300 g (1¼ cups) buttermilk

7 g (1½ tsp) baking soda

4 g (½ tsp) salt, or to taste

STEP 1: In a large mixing bowl, using a strong spatula or your hand mix together all the ingredients to create a soft, sticky dough, do not overmix.

STEP 2: Preheat the oven to 400°F (200°C) convection or 425°F (220°C) conventional. Line a large baking sheet with parchment paper.

Turn out the dough onto a well-floured counter and spread and push it with your hands to flatten it out to a ¾-inch (2-cm)-thick disk.

Use a 2½-inch (6-cm)-round cookie cutter or a similarly sized glass to cut out the biscuits: Push the cutter directly downward, then remove directly upward—do not twist it to cut or release the dough— you will lose the neat edge and the biscuits will not rise.

Place the rounds on the prepared baking sheet. They can be placed close together as they do not spread outward. You may need to use a palette knife or spatula to lift the rounds from the counter.

Once you have cut out as many rounds as possible from the dough, bring the rest of the dough together again, push it back down into a disk ¾ inch (2 cm) thick, and cut out more rounds. Keep doing this until you have cut out all of the biscuits.

STEP 3: Bake for 16 to 18 minutes, or until nicely browned.

STEP 4: Remove the biscuits from the oven and transfer them to a wire rack to cool briefly.

Top Tip:
Try adding a few seeded and chopped jalapeño chiles, or 2 teaspoons (5 g) of smoked paprika, to the dough.

Emmer and Za'atar Buttermilk Biscuits

Emmer is a wonderful ancient grain—one of the oldest, in fact, that is milled to a tasty flour. Za'atar is a fabulous Middle Eastern mixture that typically includes dried thyme, sumac, toasted sesame seeds and salt. It often contains dried marjoram and other herbs, too. It is typically mixed with olive oil and placed on the table to dunk bread into. To re-create this and offset the fact that emmer flour can become quite dry, I have included olive oil in the recipe.

PREP: To generate 85 grams (scant ½ cup) of active starter, feed all of your starter 50 grams (½ cup) of flour and 50 grams (¼ cup) of water several hours before you plan to make the dough.

Makes 15 or 16 biscuits

85 g (scant ½ cup) active starter or unfed starter

200 g (1¾ cups) white spelt flour

150 g (1¼ cups) emmer flour

300 g (1¼ cups) buttermilk

15 g (1 tbsp) olive oil

7 g (1½ tsp) baking soda

25 g (2 heaping tbsp) za'atar

4 g (½ tsp) salt, or to taste

Top Tips:

A perfect partner for za'atar is halloumi cheese. Consider using less salt as the cheese is so salty itself, and replace it with 100 grams (¾ cup) of halloumi chopped into small cubes.

If za'atar is not available, use a spice or herb blend of your choice.

STEP 1: In a large mixing bowl, using a strong spatula or your hand, mix together all the ingredients. It will come together very quickly into a soft, sticky dough.

STEP 2: Preheat the oven to 400°F (200°C) convection or 425°F (220°C) conventional. Line a large baking sheet with parchment paper.

Turn out the dough onto a well-floured counter and spread and push it with your hands to flatten it out to a ¾-inch (2-cm)-thick disk.

Use a 2½-inch (6-cm)-round cookie cutter or a similarly sized glass to cut out the biscuits: Push the cutter directly downward, then remove directly upward—do not twist it to cut or release the dough—because you will lose the neat edge and the biscuits will not rise.

Place the rounds on the prepared baking sheet. They can be placed close together as they do not spread outward. You may need to use a palette knife or spatula to lift the rounds from the counter.

Once you have cut out as many rounds as possible from the dough, bring the rest of the dough together again, push it back down into a disk ¾ inch (2 cm) thick, and cut out more rounds. Keep doing this until you have cut out all of the biscuits.

STEP 3: Bake for 16 to 18 minutes, until nicely browned.

STEP 4: Remove the biscuits from the oven and carefully transfer them to a wire rack to cool briefly.

Einkorn, Cinnamon and Cranberry Biscuits

These are a sweeter version of my buttermilk sourdough biscuits, made with cinnamon and dried fruits. The flavor and texture is like a sourdough fruit bun. For a richer taste, try replacing the oil with 30 grams (2 tablespoons) of softened unsalted butter. If you use butter in the recipe, be aware the dough may be soft and sticky.

PREP: To generate 85 grams (scant ½ cup) of active starter, feed all of your starter 50 grams (½ cup) of flour and 50 grams (¼ cup) of water several hours before you plan to make the dough.

Makes 15 or 16 biscuits

85 g (scant ½ cup) active starter or unfed starter

200 g (1¾ cups) white spelt flour, plus more for dusting

150 g (1¼ cups) whole grain einkorn flour

300 g (1¼ cups) buttermilk

120 g (1 cup) dried cranberries (or black currents, raisins, chopped dried apricots or your choice of dried fruit)

15 g (1 tbsp) rapeseed/flavorless oil

5 g (2 tsp) ground cinnamon

7 g (1½ tsp) baking soda

4 g (½ tsp) salt, or to taste

STEP 1: In a large mixing bowl, use a strong spatula or your hand to mix together all the ingredients. It does not need to be heavily mixed or kneaded.

STEP 2: Preheat the oven to 400°F (200°C) convection or 425°F (220°C) conventional. Line a large baking sheet with parchment paper.

Turn out the dough onto a well-floured counter and spread and push it with your hands to flatten it out to a ¾-inch (2-cm)-thick disk.

Use a 2½-inch (6-cm)-round cookie cutter or a similarly sized glass to cut out the biscuits: Push the cutter directly downward, then remove directly upward—do not twist it to cut or release the dough—you will lose the neat edge and the biscuits will not rise.

Place the rounds on the prepared baking sheet. They can be placed close together as they do not spread outward. You may need to use a palette knife or spatula to lift the rounds from the counter.

Once you have cut out as many rounds as possible from the dough, bring the rest of the dough together again, push it back down into a disk ¾ inch (2 cm) thick, and cut out more rounds. Keep doing this until you have cut out all of the biscuits.

STEP 3: Bake for 16 to 18 minutes, or until the biscuits are nicely browned. These will not rise as much as some of the other biscuits in this chapter, due to the added weight of the dried fruit.

STEP 4: Remove the biscuits from the oven and transfer them to a wire rack to cool briefly before eating.

SANDWICH LOAF
Sourdough Masters

Very often, I am asked whether my master recipe can be converted to make a sandwich loaf, to have slices that fit into a toaster or are perfect for sandwiches. The recipes in this chapter do just that; they can be baked in a loaf pan to create a sandwich loaf.

Use a 2-pound (900-g) pan that measures 9 x 5 inches (24 x 14 cm). Many of these pans tend to be nonstick, but I line mine with parchment paper or specially made loaf pan liners, as this makes it easier to transfer the dough into the pan. If you find that placing the doughs into the pan is a bit sticky and messy, it is normal and typical of the flour(s) used. The dough does not need to be a perfect shape at this point; it will grow and fill the pan during its final proofing and will gain a smooth surface. These loaves can also be made using the standard round banneton and pan, or, if you have them, a 11-inch (30-cm)-long oval banneton and an oval pan to create a batard.

The water content in these loaves is replaced with milk, which softens the loaf inside and out and creates a closer crumb with smaller holes, making it perfect for sandwiches as no spreads or fillings will fall through it. If you are looking for a soft-crumbed bread, this is a great solution. These recipes include loaves made with dairy and nondairy milks; these are interchangeable in all of the recipes. In the recipes that call for dairy milk, the good bacteria in your starter protects the milk in the dough during the overnight proofing; it will not go bad.

To check that the loaves are fully baked, wearing oven gloves carefully tip the pan to remove the loaf and tap the base of the loaf; if the sound is hollow, it is baked. If not, return to the oven for 5 more minutes.

Snowy White Spelt Sandwich Loaf

This recipe is perfect for anyone looking for a soft crumb paired with the beauty of sourdough in a sandwich loaf. The softness of white spelt flour benefits from being mixed with strong white bread flour and being baked in a loaf pan to give it the support that it needs. The milk softens the crust and the crumb, making it perfect for sandwiches.

PREP: Feed all of your starter at room temperature, 30 grams (¼ cup) of flour and 30 grams (⅛ cup) of water. Once it is active and bubbly and ready to use, begin your dough. Fold and cut parchment paper to fit your pan as a liner, or use a store-bought paper loaf pan liner. Have this ready to place the dough on, to lift it into the pan when the time comes.

Makes 1 standard loaf

50 g (¼ cup) active starter

300 g (1¼ cups) whole or full-fat milk, cold or at room temperature (see Note)

100 g (scant ½ cup) water

250 g (2 cups) strong white bread flour

250 g (2¼ cups) white spelt flour

7 g (1 tsp) salt, or to taste

20 g (1 tbsp) runny honey (optional)

STEP 1: In the early evening, in a large mixing bowl, mix together all the ingredients until ragged, then cover the bowl with a clean shower cap or your choice of cover and leave it on the counter for 1 hour.

STEP 2: After an hour or so, perform the first set of pulls and folds on the dough until it starts to come together into a ball. The dough will be sticky initially, but it will also be stretchy and nice to work with. Cover the bowl and leave it on the counter.

STEP 3: Over the next few hours, do 3 more sets of pulls and folds, covering the bowl after each set. The dough will be soft and stretchy and will easily come together into a soft smooth ball each time. Finish the process by completing a single round of pulls and folds before going to bed.

STEP 4: Leave the covered bowl on the counter overnight at 64 to 68°F (18 to 20°C). The dough will require between 10 and 12 hours to proof depending on whether you used cold or room-temperature milk.

STEP 5: In the morning, the dough will have grown, hopefully more than doubled, and will have a smooth surface. If it has only doubled in size, allow it 2 to 3 more hours to further proof, until tripled.

Have your pan ready and place the paper liner open on the counter. The dough will now be nicely firm. To place it in the pan, use the same pulling and folding action to gently lift and pull small handfuls of the dough from one side of the bowl into the middle in a line; turn the bowl 180 degrees and do the same on the other side so that you have a thick sausage of dough in the middle of the bowl.

(Continued)

With a wetted hand, place your whole hand over the dough, turn the bowl upside down and gently ease the dough from the bowl into your hand. Place the dough, seam side down, on the paper and slip your hand out from underneath the dough. Place the paper and dough in the pan, cover with the same shower cap and leave it on the counter. Allow the dough to proof again, letting it grow up to the level of the edge of the pan and just peek over it. This may take 2 to 3 hours, depending on the temperature of your kitchen.

STEP 6: To bake, heat the oven to 350°F (180°C) convection or 400°F (200°C) conventional. Bake the loaf for 40 minutes.

STEP 7: Once baked, gently remove the loaf from the pan and transfer it to a wire rack to cool for at least an hour before slicing. The baked loaf will come out of the oven with a crisp crust that will soften as it cools.

Note:

Whole milk produces a rich, soft, closely crumbed loaf. If you would like to make it lighter, use a lower-fat milk.

Top Tips:

Try replacing all of the water in the dough with milk for a total of 400 grams (1¾ cups) of whole milk to increase the richness and protein in the dough.

Try adding 50 grams (¼ cup) of butter for an even more enriched sourdough.

Oat Milk and Whole Wheat Sandwich Loaf

This dough creates a tangy, chewy loaf. The combination of the oat milk and whole wheat flour enhances the flavor of the sourdough, and the white spelt flour lightens the weight of the whole wheat flour. If you do not have access to oat milk, it can easily be replaced with any other milk, but oat milk is worth a try if you can find it.

PREP: Feed all of your starter at room temperature, 30 grams (¼ cup) of flour and 30 grams (⅛ cup) of water. Once it is active and bubbly and ready to use, begin your dough. Fold and cut parchment paper to fit your pan as a liner, or use a store-bought loaf pan paper liner. Have this ready to place the dough on, to lift it into the pan when the time comes.

Makes 1 standard loaf

50 g (½ cup) active starter

400 g (1¾ cups) oat milk, at room temperature or cold

250 g (2 cups) white spelt flour

250 g (2 cups) whole wheat flour

7 g (1 tsp) salt, or to taste

STEP 1: In the early evening, in a large mixing bowl, roughly mix together all the ingredients. The mixture will be sticky and soft. Leave the dough shaggy and cover the bowl with a clean shower cap or your choice of cover. Leave it on the counter for 2 hours.

STEP 2: After 2 hours, perform the first set of pulls and folds on the dough until it comes together into a nice soft ball. The dough will be sticky initially but will quickly become nice and stretchy and come together easily into a ball. Cover the bowl and leave it on the counter.

STEP 3: Perform 3 more sets of pulls and folds on the dough over the next few hours, covering the bowl after each set. The dough will be nice to work with and will easily come together into a soft ball with each handling.

Finish the process by completing a single round of pulls and folds in the bowl to pull the dough into a ball prior to going to bed.

STEP 4: Leave the covered bowl on the counter overnight at 64 to 68°F (18 to 20°C). The dough will require between 10 and 12 hours to proof, depending on whether you used cold or room-temperature milk.

STEP 5: In the morning, the dough will have grown, hopefully tripled in size, with a smooth surface.

(Continued)

Oat Milk and Whole Wheat Sandwich Loaf (Continued)

Have your loaf pan ready and place the paper liner on the counter. Repeat the pulling and folding actions to pull half of the dough gently from one side of the bowl into the middle in a line; turn the bowl 180 degrees and do the same on the other side so that you have a thick sausage of dough in the middle of the bowl. The dough will be firm and smooth.

With a wetted hand, place your whole hand over the dough, turn the bowl upside down and gently ease the dough from the bowl into your hand. Place the dough, seam side down, on the paper and slip your hand out from underneath the dough. Use the paper to lift the dough into the pan, cover it with the same shower cap and leave it on the counter.

Allow the dough to proof again, letting it grow level with the edge of the pan and just peek over the top. This may take 2 to 3 hours depending on the temperature of your kitchen.

STEP 6: Preheat the oven to 350°F (180°C) convection or 400°F (200°C) conventional. Bake the loaf for 40 minutes.

STEP 7: Once baked, remove the pan from the oven and tip the loaf from the pan. Gently remove the paper and allow the baked loaf to cool on a wire rack for at least an hour before slicing.

Coconut Milk and Rye Sandwich Loaf

The coconut milk and honey in this loaf add a subtle sweetness to the dough and the whole grain rye flour adds a lovely flavor. The dough is very sticky due to the milk and rye flour, but do not be disheartened; it will bake to a beautiful light, soft loaf. It is one of my favorite sandwich loaves. For this recipe, I use drinking coconut milk, available in cartons, rather than the coconut milk available in cans.

PREP: Feed all of your starter at room temperature, 30 grams (¼ cup) of flour and 30 grams (⅛ cup) of water. Once it is active and bubbly and ready to use, begin your dough. Fold and cut parchment paper to fit your pan as a liner, or use a store-bought loaf pan paper liner. Have this ready to place the dough on, to lift it into the pan when the time comes.

Makes 1 standard loaf

50 g (½ cup) active starter

375 g (1½ cups) drinking coconut milk, cold or at room temperature

450 g (3¾ cups) strong white bread flour

50 g (½ cup) whole grain rye flour

20 g (1 tbsp) runny honey

7 g (1 tsp) salt, or to taste

STEP 1: In the early evening, in a large mixing bowl, roughly mix together all the ingredients. The dough will be sticky from the milk and the rye flour, so I recommend a tablespoon or stiff spatula to mix the dough. Cover the bowl with a clean shower cap or your choice of cover and leave it on the counter for 1 hour.

STEP 2: After an hour or so, perform the first set of pulls and folds on the dough to bring it into a soft, sticky ball. Wet your hands to prevent the dough from sticking to your fingers. Cover the bowl and leave it on the counter.

STEP 3: Over the next few hours, perform 3 more sets of pulls and folds on the dough, covering the bowl after each set. The dough will remain sticky, but it will also be firm and will come together into a soft ball after very few actions. Do the final set before going to bed.

STEP 4: Leave the covered bowl on the counter overnight, typically 8 to 12 hours, at 64 to 68°F (18 to 20°C).

STEP 5: In the morning, the dough will have grown, typically doubled or tripled in size, with a smooth surface and a wonderful aroma. If the dough has not tripled yet, allow it a couple of more hours to continue to proof. Milk doughs take longer than those made with water.

Have your loaf pan ready and place the paper liner on the counter. Gently lift and fold small handfuls of dough from one side of the bowl into the middle in a line, using the same pulling and folding action as used previously; turn the bowl 180 degrees and do the same on the other side so that you have a thick sausage of dough in the middle of the bowl.

With a wetted hand, place your whole hand over the dough, turn the bowl upside down and gently ease the dough from the bowl into your hand. This dough is quite sticky and you may need to encourage it out of the bowl (see Note). Place the dough, seam side down, on the paper and slip your hand out from underneath the dough. Use the paper to lift the dough into the pan, cover it with the same cover and leave it on the counter.

Allow the dough to proof again, letting it grow level with the edge of the pan and just peek over the top. This may take 2 to 3 hours, depending on the temperature of your kitchen. The surface will become smooth and the dough will spread to fill the pan.

STEP 6: To bake, preheat the oven to 350°F (180°C) convection or 400°F (200°C) conventional. Bake the loaf for 40 minutes.

STEP 7: Once baked, gently remove the loaf from the pan and the paper from the loaf, and allow the baked loaf to cool on a wire rack for at least an hour before slicing.

Note:

This is a soft, sticky dough. If you find it difficult to handle, do not worry about perfect shaping; just place it on the paper as best as you can. It will even out and fill the pan during the final proofing.

Emmer and Honey Sandwich Loaf

The mixture of emmer flour with added honey in this dough produces a darker bake with an amazing depth of flavor and a slight sweetness in this sandwich loaf. The dough will be soft and sticky, and you may find it "splodges" into the pan, but it then grows and bakes to a perfect loaf, so do not worry if you find the shaping challenging. It is worth the effort!

PREP: Feed all of your starter at room temperature, 30 grams (¼ cup) of flour and 30 grams (⅛ cup) of water. Once it is active and bubbly and ready to use, begin your dough. Fold and cut parchment paper to fit your pan as a liner, or use a store-bought loaf pan paper liner. Have this ready to place the dough on, to lift it into the pan when the time comes.

Makes 1 standard loaf

50 g (¼ cup) active starter

300 g (1¼ cups) whole milk, at room temperature or cold

50 g (¼ cup) water

350 g (2¾ cups) strong white bread flour

150 g (1¼ cups) emmer flour

40 g (2 tbsp) runny honey

7 g (1 tsp) salt, or to taste

STEP 1: In the early evening, in a mixing bowl, roughly mix together all the ingredients. Leave the dough ragged, cover the bowl with a clean shower cap or your choice of cover and leave it on the counter for 2 hours.

STEP 2: After 2 hours, do the first set of pulls and folds. The dough will be sticky but it will come together into a soft ball. Cover the bowl and leave it on the counter.

STEP 3: Over the next few hours, perform 3 more sets of pulls and folds on the dough, covering the bowl after each set. The dough will remain sticky but nicely stretchy and will come together into a nice soft ball each time. Do the final set before going to bed.

STEP 4: Leave the covered bowl on the counter overnight, typically 8 to 12 hours, at 64 to 68°F (18 to 20°C).

STEP 5: In the morning, the dough will have grown, hopefully tripled in size, with a smooth surface. If the dough has not tripled yet, allow it a couple of more hours to continue to proof. Milk doughs take longer to proof than those made with water.

Have your pan ready and place the flattened paper liner on the counter. To place the dough into the pan, repeat the same pulling and folding actions that you used to build the dough and gently lift and fold small handfuls of dough from one side of the bowl into the middle in a line; turn the bowl 180 degrees and do the same on the other side so that you have a thick sausage of dough in the middle of the bowl.

With a wetted hand, place your whole hand over the dough, turn the bowl upside down and gently ease the dough from the bowl into your hand. This dough is quite sticky and you may need to encourage it out of the bowl. Place the dough, seam side down, on the paper and slip your hand out from underneath the dough. Use the paper to lift the dough into the pan, cover it with the same cover and leave it on the counter.

Allow the dough to proof again, letting it grow level with the edge of the pan and just peek over the top. This may take 2 to 3 hours, depending on the temperature of your kitchen. The surface will become smooth and the dough will spread to fill the pan.

STEP 6: To bake, preheat the oven to 350°F (180°C) convection or 400°F (200°C) conventional. Bake the loaf for 40 minutes.

STEP 7: Once the loaf is risen and browned and fully baked, gently remove the loaf from the pan and the paper from the loaf, and allow the baked loaf to cool on a wire rack for at least an hour before slicing.

Almond Milk and Khorasan Sandwich Loaf

The nuttiness of the almond milk in this dough paired with a portion of Khorasan flour adds lovely flavor as well as extra protein and nourishment to the loaf. I use a roasted almond milk; if that is not available where you are, use regular almond milk or another nut-based milk. The loaf is light and tasty and perfect for toast, sandwiches or merely pure indulgence!

PREP: Feed all of your starter at room temperature, 30 grams (¼ cup) of flour and 30 grams (⅛ cup) of water. Once it is active and bubbly and ready to use, begin your dough. Fold and cut parchment paper to fit your pan as a liner, or use a store-bought loaf pan paper liner. Have this ready to place the dough on, to lift it into the pan when the time comes.

Makes 1 standard loaf

50 g (¼ cup) active starter

375 g (1½ cups) roasted almond milk, regular almond milk or another nut milk, at room temperature or cold

400 g (3¼ cups) strong white bread flour

100 g (¾ cup) Khorasan flour

7 g (1 tsp) salt, or to taste

STEP 1: In the early evening, in a large mixing bowl, roughly mix together all the ingredients to a sticky, shaggy dough. Cover the bowl with your choice of cover and leave it on the counter for 1 hour.

STEP 2: After an hour or so, do the first set of pulls and folds until the dough comes together into a soft ball. The dough will be sticky and stretchy. Cover the bowl and leave it on the counter.

STEP 3: Over the next few hours, perform 3 more sets of pulls and folds on the dough, covering the bowl after each set. The dough will be beautifully stretchy and will come together into a soft ball each time. Cover the bowl and leave it on the counter after each set. Finish the process by completing a single round of pulls and folds in the bowl before going to bed.

STEP 4: Leave the covered bowl on the counter overnight, typically 8 to 10 hours, at 64 to 68°F (18 to 20°C).

STEP 5: In the morning, the dough will have grown, hopefully tripled in size, with a smooth surface. If you do not feel that the dough is fully proofed, cover it again and allow it to proof 2 to 3 more hours on the counter.

Have your loaf pan ready with the paper removed and flattened on the counter. The dough will be lovely and firm and smooth. To place the dough in the pan, use the same pulling and folding actions again to lift and pull small handfuls of the dough gently from one side of the bowl across the dough and into the middle in a line; turn the bowl 180 degrees and do the same on the other side so that you have a thick sausage of dough in the middle of the bowl.

With a wetted hand, place your whole hand over the dough, turn the bowl upside down and gently ease the dough from the bowl into your hand. Place the dough, seam side down, on the paper and slip your hand out from underneath the dough. Use the paper to lift the dough and paper into the pan, cover it again with the shower cap and leave it on the counter.

Allow the dough to proof again, letting it grow again to fill the pan—smooth on the top and just peeking over the edge of the pan. This may take 2 to 3 hours, depending on the temperature of your kitchen.

STEP 6: To bake, preheat the oven to 350°F (180°C) convection or 400°F (200°C) conventional. Bake for 40 minutes.

STEP 7: Once the loaf has risen and browned and fully baked, carefully remove the loaf from the pan and the paper from the loaf, and allow the baked loaf to cool on a wire rack for at least an hour before slicing.

Cooked Khorasan Grain Sandwich Loaf

I love cooked grains in any form, especially as an addition to bread. Sourdough also loves grains and doughs made with them grow beautifully. They add a lightness to the dough and a lovely chewiness and texture to the loaf. Beautifully grain-studded sourdough is one of my favorites and this milk-based sandwich loaf is fulfilling as well as tasty. Use it for sandwiches or toast; it works perfectly for both.

PREP: Feed all of your starter at room temperature, 30 grams (¼ cup) of flour and 30 grams (⅛ cup) of water. Once it is active and bubbly and ready to use, begin your dough. Fold and cut parchment paper to fit your pan as a liner, or use a store-bought loaf pan paper liner. Have this ready to place the dough on, to lift it into the pan when the time comes.

Makes 1 standard loaf

50 g (¼ cup) active starter

300 g (1¼ cups) whole milk, cold or at room temperature

100 g (scant ½ cup) water

400 g (3¼ cups) strong white bread flour

100 g (¾ cup) Khorasan flour

100 g (1 cup) cooked Khorasan grains (see page 182)

7 g (1 tsp) salt, or to taste

STEP 1: In the early evening, in a large mixing bowl, roughly mix all the ingredients, including the grains, then cover the bowl with a clean shower cap or your choice of cover and leave it on the counter for 1 to 2 hours.

STEP 2: After 1 to 2 hours, perform the first set of pulls and folds. The dough will be sticky but stretchy and will come into a soft ball. Once it comes into a ball, cover the bowl and leave it on the counter.

STEP 3: Over the next few hours, perform 3 more sets of pulls and folds on the dough, and cover it after each set. The dough will continue to be soft and stretchy and will come together into a nice ball on each handling. Complete the final set before going to bed.

STEP 4: Leave the covered bowl on the counter overnight, typically 10 to 12 hours, at 64 to 68°F (18 to 20°C).

STEP 5: In the morning, the dough will have grown, hopefully tripled in size, with a smooth surface.

Place the opened paper liner on the counter. Using the same pulling and folding action again, lift small handfuls of the dough and fold them halfway across the dough gently from one side of the bowl into the middle in a line; turn the bowl 180 degrees and do the same on the other side so that you create a thick sausage of dough.

With a wetted hand, place your whole hand over the dough, turn the bowl upside down and gently ease the dough into your hand. Place the dough, seam side down, on the paper.

Use the paper to lift the dough and paper into the pan. Do not worry if the dough does not look smooth and perfect at this point; it will proof again and will fill the pan and create a smooth surface.

Cover the pan again with the same shower cap and leave it on the counter.

Allow the dough to proof again so that it grows and fills the pan and just peeks over the edge. This may take 2 to 3 hours, depending on the temperature of your kitchen.

STEP 6: Preheat the oven to 350°F (180°C) convection or 400°F (200°C) conventional. Bake the loaf for 40 minutes.

STEP 7: Once risen and golden, carefully remove the pan from the oven, the loaf from the pan and the paper from the loaf. Place the baked loaf on a wire rack to cool for at least an hour before slicing.

THE SIMPLEST
Sourdough Rolls

These recipes share the simplest method I have ever created for making sourdough rolls, using my master recipe dough. The process utilizes the dough after its overnight proof and its time in the banneton, which allows you to bake the rolls exactly when you need them, simply and easily. The dough is cut into wedge shapes to make light, triangular-shaped bread rolls, perfect as dinner rolls, or, as in my house, for school lunch boxes.

These rolls freeze and defrost perfectly. I always have a stock of them in my freezer for lunches, to accompany a meal or for a quick snack. To freeze the rolls, store them in an airtight bag once fully cooled and freeze. To defrost, remove the rolls from the freezer and the bag and place them on a wire rack for an hour. If you froze the rolls while they were crusty, they will defrost crusty.

Alternatively, place the frozen rolls in an oven preheated to 350°F (180°C) convection or 400°F (200°C) conventional for 5 minutes, to defrost. They will be crunchy on the outside and soft and steaming on the inside.

I have created new mixtures for this chapter, but you could also use any of the dough mixtures from other chapters of the book. Simply replace the ingredients with those listed for the other recipe you want, then follow the directions in these roll recipes to proof and bake your rolls.

Top Tips:
A good dough knife is a great help for making these wedges; a nonstick one is even better.

See page 146 for step-by-step photos of the process for turning out and cutting onto the dough to make the wedges.

White Seeded Wedge Rolls

These rolls are made with my master recipe dough, using a lovely mix of strong white bread flour and white spelt flour along with pumpkin seeds to add flavor and crunch. I like to toast my seeds prior to using them in dough, it adds an extra toastiness to them. This is not a necessity, merely a preference that I happily recommend!

NOTE: These rolls do not bake to the same kind of color as a loaf; they tend to remain quite pale on the outside and fluffy on the inside.

PREP: Feed all of your starter 30 grams (¼ cup) of flour and 30 grams (⅛ cup) of water. Once it is active and bubbly and ready to use, begin your dough. Prepare a round banneton or bowl with rice flour (see page 14) and line a 12 x 16–inch (30 x 42–cm) baking pan with parchment paper.

Makes 8 rolls

50 g (¼ cup) active starter

350 g (scant 1½ cups) water

300 g (2½ cups) strong white bread flour

200 g (1¾ cups) white spelt flour

100 g (1 cup) pumpkin seeds or your favorite seeds

7 g (1 tsp) salt, or to taste

STEP 1: In the early evening, in a large mixing bowl, roughly mix together all the ingredients. Cover the bowl with a clean shower cap or your choice of cover and leave it on the counter for 1 hour.

STEP 2: After an hour or so, perform the first set of pulls and folds on the dough, stopping when it comes together into a soft ball. The dough will be silky and nice to work with, with the seeds spread throughout it. Cover the bowl and leave it on the counter.

STEP 3: Over the next few hours, do 3 more sets of pulls and folds on the dough, covering the bowl after each set. Perform the final set before going to bed.

STEP 4: Leave the covered bowl on the counter overnight, typically 8 to 10 hours, at 64 to 68°F (18 to 20°C).

STEP 5: In the morning, your bowl should be full of happy, bouncy dough, at least doubled in size. Perform one final set of pulls and folds to gently but firmly pull the dough into a loose ball. Carefully lift the dough and place it, smooth side down, in the banneton. Sprinkle extra rice flour down the sides and across the top of the dough. Cover the banneton with the same shower cap and place it in the fridge for at least 3 hours, or a maximum of 10. This way, you place it in the banneton in the morning, then bake the rolls at a perfect time for lunch or leave the bowl in the fridge for longer to bake them for dinner.

STEP 6: To bake, preheat the oven to 400°F (200°C) convection or 425°F (220°C) conventional.

Remove the cover from the banneton, then gently turn the dome of dough out onto the counter. The natural condensation that the dough has created will give its surface a layer of moisture that will prevent it from sticking to the counter. Using a nonstick dough knife or a sharp kitchen knife, cut the dough into 8 equal wedges. Gently place the wedges on the prepared pan. They will grow as they bake, so allow some space between them, but if they bake and kiss during the process, you can separate them later.

STEP 7: Bake the rolls, uncovered, for 22 minutes, or until well risen and slightly colored.

STEP 8: Once baked and risen, remove the rolls from the oven and serve once slightly cooled.

Whole Wheat and Khorasan Wedge Rolls

Light, freshly baked sourdough rolls with the flavor and goodness of whole grain flours, these rolls are a great addition to any meal, or as the meal themselves! The dough can be used whenever you are ready to bake and serve your rolls.

PREP: Feed all of your starter 30 grams (¼ cup) of flour and 30 grams (⅛ cup) of water. Once it is active and bubbly and ready to use, begin your dough. Prepare a round banneton or bowl with rice flour (see page 14) and line a 12 x 16–inch (30 x 42–cm) baking pan with parchment paper.

Makes 8 rolls

50 g (¼ cup) active starter

350 g (scant 1½ cups) water

300 g (2½ cups) strong white bread flour

150 g (1 cup) whole wheat flour

50 g (½ cup) whole grain Khorasan flour

7 g (1 tsp) salt, or to taste

STEP 1: In the early evening, in a large mixing bowl, roughly mix together all the ingredients. Cover the bowl with a clean shower cap or your choice of cover and leave it on the counter for 2 hours.

STEP 2: After the 2 hours, perform the first set of pulls and folds on the dough. Cover the bowl and leave it on the counter.

STEP 3: Over the next few hours, perform 3 more sets of pulls and folds on the dough, pulling it into a smooth ball each time. Perform the final set before going to bed. Leave the covered bowl on the counter overnight, typically 8 to 10 hours, at 64 to 68°F (18 to 20°C).

STEP 4: In the morning, your bowl should be full of happy, bouncy dough. Perform one final set of pulls and folds to gently but firmly pull the dough into a loose ball. Carefully lift the dough and place it, smooth side down, in the banneton. Sprinkle extra rice flour down the sides and across the top of the dough. Cover the banneton and place it in the fridge for at least 3 hours, or a maximum of 10.

STEP 5: When you are ready to bake, preheat the oven to 400°F (200°C) convection or 425°F (220°C) conventional. Remove the cover from the banneton and gently turn the dome of dough out onto the counter. If the dough starts to stick to the counter, you can sprinkle some water on the counter. Using a sharp kitchen knife, cut the dough into 8 equal wedges. Gently place the wedges on the prepared pan. They will grow as they bake, so allow some space between them, but if they bake and kiss during the process, you can separate them later.

STEP 6: Bake, uncovered, for 22 minutes, or until well risen.

STEP 7: Once baked and risen, remove from the oven and eat once slightly cooled.

Cooked Spelt Grain–Studded Wedge Rolls

As you may have already seen in this book, I love adding grains to sourdough, and it works equally well for rolls. The spelt grains add a great wholesome flavor and texture, and make the baked breads light and fluffy. If you have any leftover cooked grains, this is a great way to use them up and not waste them, or you can cook them for this purpose. I have used oat milk in this recipe to show an alternative to water, plus it adds a great taste and texture; however, it is not a necessity.

NOTE: The rolls do not bake to the same kind of color as a loaf; they tend to remain quite pale on the outside and fluffy on the inside.

PREP: Feed all of your starter 30 grams (¼ cup) of flour and 30 grams (⅛ cup) of water. Once it is active and bubbly and ready to use, begin your dough. Prepare a round banneton or bowl with rice flour (see page 14) and line a 12 x 16–inch (30 x 42–cm) baking pan with parchment paper.

Makes 8 rolls

50 g (¼ cup) active starter

350 g (scant 1½ cups) oat milk (see Note)

500 g (4 cups) strong white bread flour

150 g (1 cup) cooked spelt grains or any cooked grains of your choice (see page 182)

7 g (1 tsp) salt, or to taste

STEP 1: In the early evening, in a large mixing bowl, roughly mix together all the ingredients, including the grains. Cover the bowl with a clean shower cap or your cover of choice and leave it on the counter for 1 hour.

STEP 2: After an hour or so, perform the first set of pulls and folds. If your milk was cold when you added it to the dough, the dough may be stiff initially, but it will ease as you work with it. Cover the bowl and leave it on the counter.

STEP 3: Over the next few hours, perform 3 more sets of pulls and folds on the dough, covering the bowl after each set. The dough will become wonderfully stretchy and smooth with each handling. Perform the final set before going to bed.

STEP 4: Leave the covered bowl on the counter overnight, typically 8 to 10 hours, at 64 to 68°F (18 to 20°C).

(Continued)

STEP 5: In the morning, your bowl should be full of happy, bouncy dough with a smooth surface. Perform one final set of pulls and folds, once around the bowl, to pull the dough into a loose but bouncy ball. Carefully lift the dough and place it, smooth side down, in the banneton, adding extra rice flour down the sides and across the top of the dough to prevent sticking. Cover the banneton with the same shower cap and place it in the fridge. Leave the dough in the fridge for at least 3 hours, or a maximum of 10.

STEP 6: When you are ready to bake, preheat the oven to 400°F (200°C) convection or 425°F (220°C) conventional.

Remove the cover from the banneton and turn the dough out gently onto the counter. The natural condensation that the dough has created will give its surface a layer of moisture that will prevent it from sticking to the counter.

Using a nonstick dough knife, a bench scraper or a sharp kitchen knife, cut the dough into 8 equal wedges. Gently place the wedges on the prepared pan. They grow as they bake, so allow some space between them, but if they do bake and kiss during the process, you can separate them later.

STEP 7: Bake the rolls, uncovered, for 20 to 22 minutes, or until nicely risen and starting to brown.

STEP 8: Once baked, remove from the oven and eat once slightly cooled.

Note:

This is a lovely dough when prepared with oat milk, but it can be replaced with any milk of your choice or water.

Sesame Seed–Edged Emmer Wedge Rolls

The emmer flour in these rolls adds a nutty flavor and texture, and when the dough is cut into the wedge shapes, it exposes a stickiness to the sides of each wedge that is perfect for adorning with seeds.

The seeds toast while the rolls bake, without becoming bitter. Another great option is to use black sesame seeds for a more dramatic finish.

NOTE: The rolls do not bake to the same kind of color as a loaf; they tend to remain paler on the outside, but the sesame seeds will have nicely browned.

PREP: Feed all of your starter 30 grams (¼ cup) of flour and 30 grams (⅛ cup) of water and stir it well. Once it is active and bubbly and ready to use, begin your dough. Prepare a round banneton or bowl with rice flour (see page 14) and line a 12 x 16–inch (30 x 42–cm) baking pan with parchment paper.

Makes 8 rolls

50 g (¼ cup) active starter

330 g (1⅓ cups) water

350 g (2¾ cups) strong white bread flour

150 g (1¼ cups) emmer flour

7 g (1 tsp) salt, or to taste

25 g (⅛ cup) raw sesame seeds

STEP 1: In the early evening, in a large mixing bowl, roughly mix together all the ingredients, except the sesame seeds. Cover the bowl with a clean shower cap or your choice of cover and leave it on the counter for 1 hour.

STEP 2: After an hour or so, perform the first set of pulls and folds on the dough until it comes together into a loose ball. The dough will be sticky but start to become stretchy. Cover the bowl and leave it on the counter.

STEP 3: Over the next few hours, do 3 more sets of pulls and folds on the dough, covering the bowl after each set. With each set, the dough will become stretchier, less sticky and will come together into a nice ball. Perform the final set before going to bed.

STEP 4: Leave the covered bowl on the counter overnight, typically 8 to 10 hours, at 64 to 68°F (18 to 20°C).

(Continued)

STEP 5: In the morning, the dough should be at least doubled in size with a smooth surface. Perform one final set of pulls and folds to gently but firmly pull the dough into a loose ball. The dough will be stretchy and still slightly sticky, and will come together into a firm ball. Carefully lift the dough and place it, smooth side down, in the banneton. Gently sprinkle more rice flour down the sides and across the top of the dough. Cover the banneton with the same shower cap and place it in the fridge. Leave the dough in the fridge for at least 3 hours, or a maximum of 10.

STEP 6: When ready to bake, preheat the oven to 400°F (200°C) convection or 425°F (220°C) conventional.

Spread the sesame seeds on a plate. Sprinkle some water onto your countertop with your fingertips.

Remove the cover from the banneton and gently turn the dome of dough out onto the dampened counter. Using a nonstick dough knife, a bench scraper or a sharp kitchen knife, cut the dough into 8 equal wedges.

Carefully pick up each wedge and dip each long cut side of a wedge into the seeds, just touching the layer of seeds. The wedges should be nicely firm, not too soft to handle, and the seeds will happily stick to the dough. Gently place the seed-edged wedges on the prepared baking pan. They will grow as they bake, so allow some space between them, but if they bake and kiss during the process, you can separate them later.

STEP 7: Bake the rolls, uncovered, for 22 minutes, or until well risen and the seeds are slightly browned.

STEP 8: Once baked, remove the rolls from the oven and serve once slightly cooled.

Top Tip:
Dip the dough wedges into other seeds of your choice, chopped nuts, za'atar or everything bagel seasoning.

Light Rye and Chia Seed Wedge Rolls

The inclusion of the rye flour in this recipe enhances the sourdough flavor while the chia seeds add texture. This dough will be heavy, sticky and firm to work with, but it will yield beautiful, tasty baked goodies with a crusty finish and a soft crumb.

PREP: Feed all of your starter 30 grams (¼ cup) of flour and 30 grams (⅛ cup) of water. Once it is active and bubbly and ready to use, begin your dough. Prepare a round banneton or bowl with rice flour (see page 14) and line a 12 x 16–inch (30 x 42–cm) baking pan with parchment paper.

Makes 8 rolls

50 g (¼ cup) active starter

350 g (scant 1½ cups) water

350 g (2¾ cups) strong white bread flour

150 g (1½ cups) light rye flour

50 g (½ cup) chia seeds

7 g (1 tsp) salt, or to taste

STEP 1: In the early evening, in a large mixing bowl, roughly mix together all the ingredients. Cover the bowl with a clean shower cap or your choice of cover and leave it on the counter for 1 hour.

STEP 2: After an hour or so, using a stiff spatula or dough scraper as the dough will be very sticky, fold the dough into itself, around and around the bowl, until it comes together into a sticky, soft ball. Cover the bowl and leave it on the counter.

STEP 3: Over the next few hours, perform 3 sets of pulls and folds on the dough. This dough will become stretchier as you handle it, but it will remain sticky. Pull the dough into a smooth ball and cover the bowl after each set. Perform the final set before going to bed.

STEP 4: Leave the covered bowl on the counter overnight, typically 8 to 10 hours, at 64 to 68°F (18 to 20°C).

STEP 5: In the morning, the dough should be at least doubled with a smooth surface.

Perform one final set of pulls and folds to gently but firmly pull the dough into a ball. The dough will be stretchy, still quite stiff and sticky and will quickly come together into a firm, heavy ball. Carefully lift the dough and place it, smooth side down, in the banneton. Cover the banneton and place it in the fridge. Leave the dough in the fridge for at least 3 hours, or a maximum of 10.

(Continued)

Light Rye and Chia Seed Wedge Rolls (Continued)

STEP 6: When ready to bake, preheat the oven to 400°F (200°C) convection or 425°F (220°C) conventional.

Remove the cover from the banneton and gently turn the dough out onto the counter. This dough will be a firm, heavy dome. Using a nonstick dough knife or a sharp kitchen knife, cut the dough into 8 wedges; it will be easy to cut into pieces. Gently place the wedges on the prepared baking sheet with ⅜ to ¾ inch (1 to 2 cm) between them.

STEP 7: Bake the rolls, uncovered, for 22 minutes, or until nicely risen.

STEP 8: Once baked, remove the rolls from the oven and serve immediately!

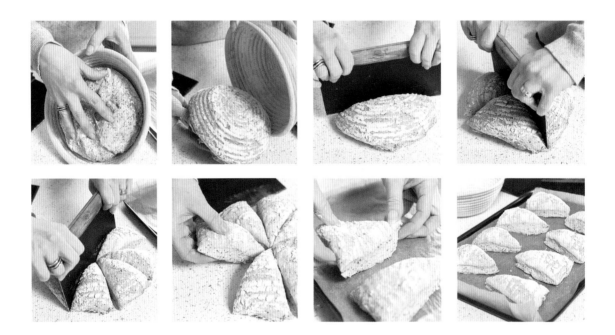

Same-Day Sourdough Wedge Rolls

By using my same-day sourdough method to make my wedge rolls, they can be prepared and ready to eat on the same day; that is, at any time from 5:30 p.m. onward. If you would like them to be freshly baked later than this, leave the banneton in the fridge until you are ready to shape and bake the dough.

Any of the wedge rolls recipes can be used with this method. Use the preparation and ingredients from the recipe of your choice.

PREP: There are two choices for your starter in this recipe: The first option is to feed your starter the night before with 60 grams (½ cup) of flour and 60 grams (¼ cup) of cold water. Leave it out overnight at 68°F (20°C) or in the fridge if it will be warmer than that; it will be ready to use in the morning. Alternatively, feed it directly from the fridge, first thing in the morning, with 60 grams (½ cup) of flour and 60 grams (¼ cup) of warm water and put it in a warm place to become active for 1 to 2 hours. Prepare a round banneton or bowl with rice flour (see page 14) and set aside a large baking pan with a lid, plus parchment paper.

Makes 8 rolls

100 g (½ cup) active starter

325 g (1⅓ cups) warm water, warm to the touch, not hot

300 g (2½ cups) strong white bread flour

200 g (1⅔ cups) whole wheat flour

7 g (1 tsp) salt, or to taste

9:30 A.M. / STEP 1: In a large mixing bowl, mix together all the ingredients, stirring well initially and finishing off by giving the mixture a few good squeezes. It may be sticky due to the warm water and extra starter. Leave it roughly mixed. Cover the bowl with a clean shower cap or your choice of cover and place it in a warm spot in your kitchen or home, ideally around 77°F (25°C).

You can use the oven with the oven light on only and the door propped open. With my oven, this provides a constant temperature of 77°F (25°C). (If I close the door, it goes up to 99°F [37°C], which is far too hot, even for the shortened proofing time.) If you have a proofing box or warming drawer, it would be ideal for the job. Use a thermometer to monitor the temperature and make sure it does not exceed 77°F (25°C).

10:00 A.M. / STEP 2: Perform the first set of pulls and folds on the dough: Pick up a small handful of the dough, pull it up and across the dough, turn the bowl slightly and repeat the action, all the way around the bowl several times; it may require more than normal handling at this point due to the stickiness of the dough. Perform 20 to 25 pulls and folds at this point.

Cover the bowl again and place it back in the warmth.

(Continued)

10:30 A.M. / STEP 3: Perform the next set of pulls and folds, repeating the same actions again; the dough should be nice and stretchy and bouncy, and come into a nice smooth, soft ball.

Place the covered bowl back in the warmth.

11:00 A.M. / STEP 4: Perform the last set of pulls and folds; the dough should come into a nice smooth bouncy ball.

Place the covered bowl back in the warmth for the next 3 hours.

2:00 P.M. / STEP 5: By now, the dough should have grown to at least double its original size. It may be soft from the warm proofing but it should not be floppy.

Using the same actions as for the earlier pulls and folds, pull the dough gently together into a soft, bouncy ball. Do not be heavy handed at this point; work gently to protect what your starter has done.

Place the dough, smooth side down, in the banneton. Add extra rice flour around it if necessary to ensure it is not sticking anywhere, and add more across the top.

Cover the banneton with the shower cap and place it in the fridge.

Leave the dough in the fridge for 3 hours or longer, depending on your plans.

5:00 P.M. / STEP 6: When ready to bake, preheat the oven to 400°F (200°C) convection or 425°F (220°C) conventional.

Remove the cover from the banneton and gently turn the dough out onto the counter. This dough will be a firm heavy dome. Using a nonstick dough knife or a sharp kitchen knife, cut the dough into 8 wedges; it will be firm and easy to cut into pieces. Gently place the wedges on the prepared baking sheet.

STEP 7: Bake the rolls, uncovered, for 22 minutes, or until slightly browned.

STEP 8: Once baked, remove the rolls from the oven and serve immediately!

COILED FILLED
Sourdough Rolls

These rolls are a great addition to any dinner table. They taste great as well as look great. They also provide another way to use the master recipe dough. The coils are created by "laminating" the dough, which is basically a fancy word for creating layers, and filling the dough with ingredients and flavors of your choice. I have included some of my favorite choices, but the possibilities are endless. They are also great fun to make, especially with children.

The process uses the master recipe dough (see page 27). Following the overnight proofing, it is stretched out, sprinkled with the fillings, rolled up, cut into pieces and baked. When you stretch out the dough, it is amazing—you can see the structure of the dough and the bubbles all the way through it. Stretching it also shows just how forgiving sourdough can be. Resist the temptation to use a rolling pin for these recipes; the action will squash all the bubbles and carefully crafted air pockets out of the dough.

Note:

After the overnight proofing, the doughs can be used immediately. Alternatively, if you want the rolls for later in the day, without performing any pulls and folds, place the covered bowl of proofed dough in the fridge to stop the proofing process. Store in the fridge for up to 6 hours. One hour before you are ready to make the rolls, take the dough from the fridge. This allows it to warm up to room temperature and therefore it will be easier to handle.

Mixed Toasted Seeds Swirls

These lovely swirls, made with dough that includes whole wheat flour, are studded with toasted seeds. They are tasty, crunchy and full of goodness! Use your favorite seeds or a mix of a few kinds to create a wholesome, filling roll.

PREP: Feed all of your starter with 30 grams (¼ cup) of your flour and 30 grams (⅛ cup) of water. Once it is active and bubbly and ready to use, begin your dough. Line a 12 x 16–inch (30 x 42–cm) baking pan with parchment paper.

Makes 8 rolls

50 g (¼ cup) active starter

350 g (scant 1½ cups) water

250 g (2 cups) strong white bread flour

250 g (2 cups) whole wheat flour

7 g (1 tsp) salt, or to taste

100 g (1 cup) toasted seeds of your choice (see Top Tip)

STEP 1: In the early evening, in a large mixing bowl, roughly mix together all the ingredients, except the seeds. Cover with a clean shower cap or your choice of cover and leave it on the counter for 2 hours.

STEP 2: After 2 hours, perform the first set of pulls and folds on the dough; it will be firm but stretchy. Once the dough comes into a ball, cover the bowl and leave it on the counter.

STEP 3: Over the next few hours, perform 3 more sets of pulls and folds on the dough, covering the bowl after each set, completing a final round of pulls and folds before going to bed.

STEP 4: Leave the covered bowl on the counter overnight at 64 to 68°F (18 to 20°C) for 8 to 10 hours.

STEP 5: The next morning, the dough should have grown by at least double, hopefully even more, with a smooth surface and textured underneath. Use immediately or save for later (see Note, page 151).

Step 6: When ready to bake, preheat your oven to 400°F (200°C) convection or 425°F (220°C) conventional.

Sprinkle your kitchen counter with water. Using a bowl scraper or your hands, gently ease the bubbly risen dough from the bowl onto the counter. With your fingertips, start to stretch the dough out; gently pull and stretch it, pushing the dough outward from the middle if necessary, being careful not to make any holes, until it forms a rectangle that measures about 16 x 20 inches (40 x 50 cm) with an even thickness all over. It may take a little while to stretch out, as the dough will want to keep bouncing back, but it will give in eventually.

Once the dough is stretched out, spread the seeds evenly over the dough, all the way to the edges. Starting from one of the short sides of the dough, roll up the dough until it is an even sausage. Using a dough knife or sharp knife, cut the dough into 8 equal pieces. Wet your fingers to lift and place them, cut side down, on the prepared pan with space between for them to grow as they bake. Bake for 20 to 22 minutes, or until risen and browned.

STEP 7: Once baked, remove the rolls from the oven and allow them to cool briefly, then serve.

Top Tip:
Try replacing or mixing the seeds with your favorite chopped nuts.

Cheese and Pesto Emmer Roll-Ups

What can I say, except . . . yum! These are so tasty! Imagine melted cheese baked with your favorite pesto oozing from tasty rolls made with emmer flour; that is these lovely rolls. I like mine made with strong Cheddar cheese and basil or tomato pesto. The struggle is not to eat them all as soon as they are baked!

For different flavors, try replacing the pesto with tomato or red pepper pesto, harissa, pizza sauce or chipotle in adobo sauce.

PREP: Feed all of your starter 30 grams (¼ cup) of flour and 30 grams (⅛ cup) of water. Once it is active and bubbly and ready to use, begin your dough. Line a 12 x 16–inch (30 x 42–cm) baking pan with parchment paper.

Makes 8 rolls

50 g (¼ cup) active starter

300 g (scant 1¼ cups) water

400 g (3¼ cups) strong white bread flour

100 g (¾ cup) emmer flour

7 g (1 tsp) salt, or to taste

100 g (⅓ cup) basil, tomato or red pepper pesto

200 g (1½ cups) grated cheese of your choice (a stronger-flavored cheese works best)

STEP 1: In the early evening, in a large mixing bowl, roughly mix together all the ingredients, except the pesto and cheese, leaving the dough shaggy. Cover the bowl with a clean shower cap or your choice of cover and leave it on the counter for 1 hour.

STEP 2: After an hour or so, perform the first set of pulls and folds on the dough; it will be sticky at this point, but stretchy. Cover the bowl and leave it on the counter.

STEP 3: Over the next few hours, complete 3 more sets of pulls and folds on the dough, covering the bowl after each set. The dough will be nicely stretchy and will easily come together into a firm ball each time. Complete the final set before going to bed.

STEP 4: Leave the covered bowl on the counter overnight, typically 8 to 10 hours, at 64 to 68°F (18 to 20°C).

STEP 5: The next morning, the dough is now ready to be used to make the rolls. Use immediately or save for later (see Note, page 151).

STEP 6: When ready to bake, preheat the oven to 400°F (200°C) convection or 425°F (220°C) conventional.

Sprinkle water over your kitchen counter. Using a bowl scraper or your hands, gently ease the bubbly risen dough from the bowl onto the counter. Use your fingertips to start stretching and pushing out the dough, until it becomes a rectangle that measures about 16 x 20 inches (40 x 50 cm) with an even thickness all over. The dough will want to pull back as your stretch it; continue to pull it gently, careful not to make holes in the dough.

Dot teaspoonfuls of pesto over the stretchy dough. Spread the grated cheese evenly over the dough, right up to the edges. Roll up the dough from one of the longer edges toward the other to make an even roll of dough. Using a dough knife or sharp knife, cut the dough into 8 equal pieces. Wet your fingers to lift and place them, cut side down, on the prepared pan with space between for them to grow as they bake. They can also be placed slightly closer together as in the photo, to create a pull-apart bread. Bake for 20 to 22 minutes, or until browned.

STEP 7: Once baked and smelling fabulous, remove the rolls from the oven and let them sit briefly on the hot pan before serving. Best eaten freshly baked.

Almond Butter and Banana Khorasan Coils

I am a huge nut butter fan—any nut works for me! In these coils, the warm almond butter, partnered with the hot chunks of banana and the joy of sourdough, creates pure heavenly wonders! The flavor of sourdough is enhanced by the added nuttiness from the Khorasan flour. While I love almond butter in these coils, feel free to try your own favorite nut butter instead.

PREP: Feed all of your starter with 30 grams (¼ cup) of flour and 30 grams (⅛ cup) of water. Once it is active and bubbly and ready to use, begin your dough. Line a 12 x 16–inch (30 x 42–cm) baking pan with parchment paper.

Makes 8 rolls

50 g (¼ cup) active starter

325 g (1⅓ cups) water

300 g (2¼ cups) strong white bread flour

200 g (1¾ cups) Khorasan flour

7 g (1 tsp) salt, or to taste

2 medium or 1 large ripe banana

48 g (3 tbsp) almond butter, or your favorite nut butter

STEP 1: In the early evening, in a large mixing bowl, roughly mix together all the ingredients, except the banana and nut butter, leaving the dough ragged. Cover the bowl with a clean shower cap or your choice of cover and leave it on the counter for 2 hours.

STEP 2: After 2 hours or so, perform the first set of pulls and folds on the dough; it will be a nicely stretchy dough to work with. Cover the bowl and leave it on the counter.

STEP 3: Over the next few hours, perform 3 more sets of pulls and folds on the dough, covering the bowl after each set, completing the final set before going to bed.

STEP 4: Leave the covered bowl on the counter overnight, typically 8 to 10 hours, at 64 to 68°F (18 to 20°C).

STEP 5: The next morning, the dough is now ready to be used to make the rolls. Use immediately or save for later (see Note, page 151).

STEP 6: When ready to bake, preheat your oven to 400°F (200°C) convection or 425°F (220°C) conventional.

Sprinkle your kitchen counter with water. Using a bowl scraper or your hands, gently ease the bubbly risen dough from the bowl onto the counter. Using your fingertips, gently push and stretch the dough out to a rectangle that measures about 16 x 20 inches (40 x 50 cm) with an even thickness all over.

Peel and cut the banana(s) lengthwise, then into slices. Give your nut butter a good stir to loosen it up. Dot the dough with the banana pieces and spoon and/or drizzle the nut butter evenly over all. Roll up the dough, starting along one short side, rolling it firmly toward the other, without squashing it, to make a nice sausage. Then, using a dough knife or sharp knife, cut the dough into 8 equal pieces. Wet your fingertips to lift and place them, cut side down, on the tray with space between for them to grow. Bake for 20 to 22 minutes, or until browned.

STEP 7: Once baked, remove the rolls from the oven and let them sit briefly. Serve warm.

Mixed Dried Fruit, Nut and Seed Einkorn Coils

These coils are packed with your choice of dried fruits, nuts and seeds. I used raisins, cranberries, pumpkin seeds and mixed chopped nuts. The whole grain einkorn flour in this dough provides a great wholesome flavor, while the dried fruits add sweetness and the nuts and seeds add crunch. I rolled this dough slightly differently from the previous three recipes, and cut it into twelve to make smaller rolls. This technique can be applied to any of the other coil doughs.

PREP: Feed all of your starter with 30 grams (¼ cup) of your flour and 30 grams (⅛ cup) of water. Once it is active and bubbly and ready to use, begin your dough. Line a 12 x 16–inch (30 x 42–cm) baking pan with parchment paper.

Makes 12 rolls

50 g (¼ cup) active starter

325 g (1⅓ cups) water

375 g (3 cups) strong white bread flour

125 g (1 cup) whole grain einkorn flour

7 g (1 tsp) salt, or to taste

100 g (1 cup) mixed dried fruits

100 g (¾ cup) chopped nuts and seeds

STEP 1: In the early evening, in a large mixing bowl, mix together all the ingredients, except the dried fruits, nuts and seeds, leaving the dough shaggy. Cover the bowl with a clean shower cap or your choice of cover and leave it on the counter for 2 to 3 hours.

STEP 2: After 2 to 3 hours, perform the first set of pulls and folds on the dough; it will be nicely stretchy and slightly spongy. Cover the bowl and leave it on the counter.

STEP 3: Over the next few hours, complete 3 more sets of pulls and folds on the dough, covering the bowl after each set. Finish the process by completing a single round of pulls and folds, bringing the dough back into a ball, before going to bed.

STEP 4: Leave the covered bowl on the counter overnight, typically 8 to 10 hours, at 64 to 68°F (18 to 20°C).

STEP 5: The next morning, the dough will be nicely doubled in size. It is now ready to be used to make the rolls. Use immediately or save for later (see Note, page 151).

STEP 6: When ready to bake, preheat the oven to 400°F (200°C) convection or 425°F (220°C) conventional. Sprinkle your kitchen counter with water. Using a bowl scraper or your hands, gently ease the bubbly risen dough from the bowl onto the counter. Using your fingertips, gently push and stretch the dough out to a rectangle that measures about 16 x 24 inches (40 x 60 cm).

Spread the dried fruit, nuts and seeds evenly over the dough, right up to the edges as close as possible. Roll up the dough from one long side to the other, then using a dough knife or sharp knife, cut the dough into 12 pieces, as similarly sized as possible. Wet your fingertips to lift and place the pieces, cut side down, on the prepared pan with space between for them to grow. Bake for 18 to 20 minutes, or until risen and browned. Note that if the dried fruit on top starts to brown, cover the pan with another pan or foil, to stop them from burning.

STEP 7: Once baked, remove the rolls from the oven and let them cool slightly before serving them warm and fabulous.

SWAP THE *Water*

These loaves are all made by replacing the water with other liquids in the dough. It is a great way to experiment and see what you can create; you will also discover how the dough behaves when another liquid is used and how the baked loafs then differ.

For example, the bread made with buttermilk produces a lovely soft loaf with all of the sourdough flavor, whereas the beer adds a richness and color. Using other liquids is a great way to introduce new tastes and textures, as well as to use up leftovers, such as water in which vegetables or beans have been cooked. Dough loves the carbohydrates and sugars in their liquid.

Have fun with your dough!

Buttermilk White Spelt Master Loaf

This loaf is made using buttermilk instead of water in the dough. Because it contains white spelt flour, the dough may be sticky to work with and feel heavy, but the loaf will be tasty and soft, almost as if enriched. If you are looking for the benefits and flavor of sourdough in a fluffy loaf, this is the one for you.

This loaf is perfect for sandwiches, as the freshly baked bread is soft with a tight crumb (no holes for anything to fall through), and the next day, it is still soft enough to eat fresh, or makes wonderful toast.

This loaf will bake darker than loaves made with water, and as it bakes, it will not blossom and grow as much as dough made with water does.

PREP: Feed all of your starter 30 grams (¼ cup) of flour and 30 grams (⅛ cup) of water. Once it is active and bubbly and ready to use, begin your dough. Prepare a round banneton or bowl with rice flour (see page 14) and set aside a large baking pan with a lid, plus parchment paper.

Makes 1 standard loaf

50 g (¼ cup) active starter

400 g (1⅔ cups) buttermilk, at room temperature (see Top Tip)

300 g (2½ cups) strong white bread flour

200 g (1¾ cups) white spelt flour

7 g (1 tsp) salt, or to taste

STEP 1: In the early evening, in a large mixing bowl, roughly mix together all the ingredients, leaving the mixture ragged. This dough will be quite stiff. Cover the bowl with a clean shower cap or your choice of cover and leave it on the counter for 1 hour.

STEP 2: After an hour or so, start to work with the dough; it will be stiff initially and you may need to fold it in on itself rather than pull and fold it for this first handling. Do it around the bowl until it comes together into a nice firm ball, then stop. Cover the bowl and leave it on the counter.

STEP 3: Over the next few hours, perform 3 more sets of pulls and folds on the dough. It will become stretchier as you work with it and you will be able to smell the buttermilk in the mixture.

STEP 4: Cover the bowl and leave it on the counter overnight, typically 8 to 10 hours, at 64 to 68°F (18 to 20°C). (If your buttermilk was cold, directly from the fridge, your dough may need a couple of hours longer.)

(Continued)

STEP 5: In the morning, the dough will have grown, ideally at least double its original size with a smooth, ballooned surface. Pull the dough into a ball; the dough will be firm and will not need much handling to form a ball. Place the dough, smooth side down, in the banneton, sprinkle extra rice flour down the sides and across the top of the dough, cover with the same shower cap and place it in the fridge for at least 3 hours.

STEP 6: After 3 to 10 hours in the fridge, preheat the oven to 425°F (220°C) convection or 450°F (230°C) conventional. For how to bake from a cold start, visit page 30.

Have your parchment paper and pan ready. Remove the cover from the banneton, then place the paper over the top of the banneton and the pan upside down over the top of them both. With one hand under the banneton and one on the pan, turn it all over together to turn the dough into the pan.

Using a bread lame, score the dome of the dough cleanly and firmly; it will be a nice firm, smooth dough and a joy to score. Place the lid on the pan and bake for 50 minutes. After 50 minutes, if you would like more color on your loaf, place the pan back in the hot oven, minus the lid, for 5 to 10 minutes.

STEP 7: Once baked, carefully remove the loaf from the pan and allow the baked loaf to cool on a wire rack for at least an hour before slicing.

Top Tip:

As a variation, try replacing the buttermilk with 350 grams (1½ cups) of whey, for a lighter loaf with a hint of cheese flavor.

Potato Water and Rye Master Loaf

This loaf is made using the water left over from boiling potatoes. The dough loves the starch in the water, and it is a great way to use the water rather than throw it away. The dough becomes smooth and grows beautifully, and the baked loaf is light and nicely chewy.

To obtain potato water, whenever you are boiling some potatoes, collect the water when you drain them and allow it to cool. Store, covered, in the fridge for up to a week until you are ready to use it, then take it out of the fridge to warm up.

PREP: Feed all of your starter with 30 grams (¼ cup) of flour and 30 grams (⅛ cup) of water. Once it is active and bubbly and ready to use, begin your dough. Prepare a round banneton or bowl with rice flour (see page 14) and gather a large baking pan with a lid and parchment paper.

Makes 1 standard loaf

50 g (¼ cup) active starter

350 g (scant 1½ cups) potato cooking water, at room temperature (see headnote)

450 g (3½ cups) strong white bread flour

50 g (½ cup) dark rye flour

7 g (1 tsp) salt, or to taste

STEP 1: In the early evening, in a large mixing bowl, roughly mix together all the ingredients, leaving the mixture shaggy. Cover the bowl with a clean shower cap or your choice of cover and leave it on the counter for 1 hour.

STEP 2: After an hour or so, perform the first set of pulls and folds on the dough. The dough will be sticky from the rye flour in the mixture. When the dough comes into a nice ball, cover the bowl again.

STEP 3: Over the next few hours, perform 3 more sets of pulls and folds on the dough, covering the bowl after each set. The dough will become smoother with each handling. Finish the process by completing a set of pulls and folds, bringing the dough back into a ball, before going to bed.

STEP 4: Leave the covered bowl on the counter overnight, typically 8 to 10 hours, at 64 to 68°F (18 to 20°C).

STEP 5: In the morning, the dough should have doubled in size, with a smooth surface. Do a final set of pulls and folds to pull the dough into a firm ball, then place the dough, smooth side down, in your prepared banneton, adding an extra sprinkle of rice flour down the sides and across the top of the dough. Cover the banneton with the same shower cap and place it in the fridge for at least 3 hours.

(Continued)

STEP 6: After 3 to 10 hours in the fridge, preheat the oven to 425°F (220°C) convection or 450°F (230°C) conventional. For how to bake from a cold start, see page 30.

Remove the cover from the banneton, then place the parchment paper over the top of the banneton and the pan upside down over the top of them both. With one hand under the banneton and one on the pan, turn it all over together to turn the dough into the pan.

Using a bread lame or razor blade, score the dome. I scored my loaf with a 6-point star. Place the lid on the pan and bake for 50 minutes. After 50 minutes, if you would like more color on your loaf, place the pan back in the hot oven, minus the lid, for 5 to 10 minutes.

STEP 7: Once baked, carefully remove the loaf from the pan and allow the baked loaf to cool on a wire rack for at least an hour before slicing.

Top Tip:

As a variation, try using water leftover from cooking other vegetables or beans and see the different colors and flavors it creates.

Sweet Potato and Spelt Master Loaf

I created this loaf by throwing some leftover roasted sweet potato into my dough and the outcome was glorious. This lovely loaf is made using the water from boiling sweet potato and includes sweet potato in the dough. The water adds color to the dough and the sweet potato provides flavor and a lovely moisture, as well as the benefit of adding a vegetable to your bread. (A perfect way to add secret vegetables!) The baked loaf will have a thin, soft crust and a moist, chewy interior. It is great for making sandwiches as it is so wonderfully soft.

This dough is a pleasure to work with, it grows beautifully and the wild yeast in the starter loves the natural sugars in the sweet potato and starch in the water.

PREP: Feed all of your starter with 30 grams (¼ cup) of your flour and 30 grams (⅛ cup) of water. Once it is active and bubbly and ready to use, begin your dough. Prepare a round banneton or bowl with rice flour (see page 14) and set aside a large baking pan with a lid, plus parchment paper.

Makes 1 standard loaf

200 g (7 oz) sweet potato (see Top Tip)

At least 350 g (scant 1½ cups) water

50 g (¼ cup) active starter

300 g (2½ cups) strong white bread flour

200 g (1¾ cups) white spelt flour

7 g (1 tsp) salt, or to taste

COOK THE SWEET POTATO: Peel the sweet potato and cut it into 1-inch (2.5-cm) chunks. If you have more than 200 grams (7 oz), just cook all of it; you can use 200 grams for the recipe and enjoy the extra on its own.

In a medium saucepan, combine the sweet potato chunks with more than 350 grams (1¾ cups) of cold water. Bring the water to a boil, then place a lid loosely over the pan and lower the heat to a simmer. Simmer the sweet potato for 10 minutes, or until it is cooked and soft, but not breaking up.

Drain the water, catching and reserving 350 grams (scant 1½ cups) for the recipe.

Allow both the water and sweet potato to cool before using.

STEP 1: In the evening, in a large mixing bowl, roughly mix together all the ingredients. The sweet potato chunks do not need to be fully mixed in or broken down. Cover the bowl with a clean shower cap or your choice of cover and leave it on the counter for 1 hour.

STEP 2: After about an hour, perform the first set of pulls and folds on the dough, covering the bowl after each set. As you work with the dough, the sweet potato will break up and become incorporated into the dough. Once the dough comes together into a nice ball, cover the bowl and leave it on the counter.

(Continued)

STEP 3: Over the next few hours, perform 3 more sets of pulls and folds on the dough. The dough will be nice to handle—stretchy, happy and bouncy. With each handling, the sweet potato will break down and mix in more thoroughly. Finish the process by completing a single round of pulls and folds before going to bed.

STEP 4: Leave the covered bowl on the counter overnight, typically 8 to 10 hours, at 64 to 68°F (18 to 20°C).

STEP 5: In the morning, the dough will have grown, typically at least double its original size.

Use the same pulling and folding motion to gently but firmly pull the dough into a soft ball. This dough will be nicely resistant; you will be able to make a lovely bouncy ball. Place it, smooth side down, in the banneton. Sprinkle some extra rice flour down the sides of the banneton and across the top of the dough. Cover the banneton with the same shower cap and place it in the fridge for at least 3 hours. (This dough often continues to grow in the fridge to fill the banneton.)

STEP 6: After 3 to 10 hours in the fridge, preheat the oven to 425°F (220°C) convection or 450°F (230°C) conventional. For how to bake from a cold start, see page 30.

Remove the cover from the banneton, then place your parchment paper over the top of the banneton and the pan base upside down over the top of them both. With one hand under the banneton and one on the pan, turn it all over together to turn the dough into the pan.

Using a bread lame or razor blade, score the dome of dough. I scored the loaf with an X. Put the lid on the pan and bake for 50 minutes. After 50 minutes, if you would like more color on your loaf, place the pan back in the hot oven, minus the lid, for 5 to 10 minutes.

STEP 7: Once baked, remove the loaf from the pan and allow the baked loaf to cool on a wire rack for at least an hour before slicing.

Top Tip:

For a different flavor, try replacing the sweet potato with butternut squash or pumpkin, and try using the cooking water from them, too.

Beer and Spent Grains Master Loaf

Beer and bread share a long history, and this recipe has all of the history rolled into one loaf. The beer adds great extra flavor. Use your favorite beer, ale or cider and see which you like the best. A good, strongly flavored beer works well. Spent grains are grains that have been used in the process of making beer. These are typically malted barley grains that are mashed during the beer-making process to extract the protein, sugar and nutrients from the grains, hence leaving them "spent."

Spent grains are the biggest waste product from making beer; typically, they tend to become animal feed after being removed from the beer, but they are fully edible and very tasty, so this is a great way to use them differently. They are wonderful when added to dough and baked into bread. If you have a brewery close by, ask whether they can spare some for you to experiment with—that is what I did! When you collect the grains, they will be wet; you can use some in dough as they are and store any unused spent grains in the fridge.

The mixture of beer, whole grain spelt flour and spent grains in this dough produces a chewy texture and a wonderful deep flavor. If you are not able to obtain any spent grains, make the recipe without them to still enjoy the benefit of using the beer in the dough. Or you can try replacing the spent grain with cooked and cooled spelt or einkorn grains.

PREP: Feed all of your starter with 30 grams (¼ cup) of flour and 30 grams (⅛ cup) of water. Once it is active and bubbly and ready to use, begin your dough. Prepare a round banneton or bowl with rice flour (see page 14) and set aside a large baking pan with a lid, plus parchment paper.

Makes 1 standard loaf

50 g (¼ cup) active starter

350 g (1½ cups) your choice of beer, ideally a malty ale

300 g (2½ cups) strong white bread flour

200 g (1¾ cups) whole grain spelt flour

100 g (1 cup) wet spent grains

7 g (1 tsp) salt, or to taste

STEP 1: In the early evening, in a large mixing bowl, roughly mix together all the ingredients. Cover the dough with a clean shower cap or your choice of cover and leave it on the counter for 2 hours.

STEP 2: After about 2 hours, perform the first set of pulls and folds on the dough. The dough may feel stiff and sticky initially, but it will come together into a ball. Cover the bowl again and leave it on the counter.

STEP 3: Over the next few hours, perform 3 more sets of pulls and folds on the dough, covering it after each set. The dough will start to become spongy and you will be able to smell the beer as you move the dough. Finish the process by completing a single round of pulls and folds in the bowl, bringing the dough back into a ball, before going to bed.

STEP 4: Leave the covered bowl on the counter overnight, typically 8 to 10 hours, at 64 to 68°F (18 to 20°C).

(Continued)

Beer and Spent Grains Master Loaf (Continued)

STEP 5: In the morning, the dough will have grown, possibly double in size. Do a single round of pulls and folds on the dough to pull it into a firm ball, then lift it gently and place it, smooth side down, in the banneton. Cover the banneton with the same shower cap and place it in the fridge for at least 3 hours.

STEP 6: After 3 to 10 hours in the fridge, preheat the oven to 425°F (220°C) convection or 450°F (230°C) conventional. For how to bake from a cold start, see page 30.

Remove the cover from the banneton, then place the parchment paper over the banneton and the pan base upside down over the top of them both. With one hand under the banneton and one on the pan, turn it all over together to turn the dough into the pan.

Using a bread lame or razor blade, score the dome of the dough. I scored my loaf with a geometric pattern. Put the lid on the pan and bake for 50 minutes. After 50 minutes, if you would like more color on your loaf, place the pan back in the hot oven, minus the lid, for 5 to 10 minutes.

STEP 7: Once baked, remove the loaf from the pan and allow the baked loaf to cool on a wire rack for at least an hour before slicing.

Top Tips:

If the spent grains you have are very wet, spread them out to a thin, even layer on a baking sheet lined with parchment paper and let them sit for a day or two to dry out slightly. Or store them in a colander set over a bowl. Allow the liquid to drain to the bottom bowl so that you can scoop grains out from the top.

For longer storage, keep the spent grains on the baking sheet to dry out completely. This will take 2 to 3 days, depending on the temperature of your kitchen. Alternatively, dry them in the oven set to a low heat, 300°F (150°C). You can then use the grains like that, or toast some for 5 to 10 minutes for even more flavor at 350°F (180°C). They do not take long to toast in the oven; you just need to watch them and move them around a few times so that the grains on the edges do not burn.

You can then use these dried and toasted grains whole in your dough, or grind some to make a flour and add some to your usual sourdough mix. I usually add 5 to 10 grams (2 to 3 tablespoons); they're really light, so even 5 grams (2 tablespoons) is quite a lot and adds a lovely flavor to your bread.

CRACKERS

Crackers are a great way to use your starter differently, and to make a fast recipe. They are open to lots of options, using whatever ingredients take your fancy. These are perfect to make with discarded starter from making new starters, or by feeding your starter especially for the occasion. The starter adds flavor rather than volume in these recipes.

Top Tips:

Each recipe has a slightly different timetable, and each can be swapped with another based on the timing you prefer.

This is an ideal way to use starter that you fed intending to make a loaf and ran out of time.

The crackers freeze and defrost perfectly. Freeze, once cooled, in an airtight bag or container; defrost, uncovered, in a single layer on a wire rack for 5 minutes.

Speedy Seed and Oat Crackers

Lovely seeded beauties! These crackers are made by mixing up a dough, letting it sit briefly and then using it immediately, whereas the following cracker recipes have longer resting times. This dough can be mixed and ready to roll out and bake in the time it takes to heat your oven.

PREP: Feed all of your starter 60 grams (½ cup) of flour and 60 grams (¼ cup) of water. Allow it to become active and ready to use.

Makes 16 to 20 crackers

100 g (½ cup) active or unfed spare starter

50 g (scant ½ cup) rolled oats

50 g (scant ½ cup) strong white bread flour, plus more for dusting

40 g (¼ cup) mixed seeds (pumpkins seeds, sunflower seeds, flaxseeds) or a single type of seed (see Top Tip)

25 g (⅛ cup) water

30 g (2 tbsp) olive oil

10 g (1½ tsp) runny honey

3 g (½ tsp) salt, or to taste

Top Tip:
Toasting the seeds prior to use gives them a lovely crunch and a deeper flavor. Allow them to cool before using them.

STEP 1: In a mixing bowl, mix together all the ingredients to form a stiff dough, bringing it together with your hands, large spoon or stiff spatula. Let the mixture sit for 30 minutes.

STEP 2: Preheat the oven to 350°F (180°C) convection or 375°F (190°C) conventional. Line a baking sheet with parchment paper and set aside.

Dust your counter with a little flour and turn the dough out of the bowl and onto the counter. Use a rolling pin to roll out the dough to ⅛ inch (3 mm) thick. You may need flour on the rolling pin, too, to stop the dough from sticking and to keep moving your dough around as you roll it out, so that it does not stick to the counter.

Cut out rounds from the dough with a 2½-inch (6-cm) cookie or biscuit cutter. Alternatively, use a pizza cutter or sharp knife to cut the dough into 2½-inch (6-cm) squares. Use a thin spatula to lift the crackers as they will be delicate, and place the squares on the prepared baking pan. They can be placed quite close together, as the crackers do not spread sideways as they bake. Bring the rest of the dough together again, roll it out and cut more crackers from it until you have used all of the dough. Prick each cracker with a fork 2 to 3 times to prevent them from puffing up as they bake.

STEP 3: Bake for 7 minutes on one side, then remove the pan from the oven, carefully turn the crackers over with a fork and a small metal spatula, return the pan to the oven, then bake for another 7 minutes.

STEP 4: Remove the crackers from the oven and transfer them to a wire rack to cool for a few minutes. When first baked, the crackers will be slightly soft and chewy; they will crisp up as they cool. These crackers are great to eat as soon as they have cooled slightly. Store any leftovers in an airtight container.

Whole Wheat Sesame and Oat Crackers

This cracker recipe allows you to mix the dough and leave it to sit until you are ready to use it. The sesame seeds with the whole grain flour plus the oats works perfectly, and adds flavor, texture and cohesion to a dough packed full of goodness!

PREP: Feed all of your starter 60 grams (½ cup) of flour and 60 grams (¼ cup) of water. Allow it to become active and ready to use.

Makes 16 to 20 crackers

100 g (½ cup) active or unfed spare starter

50 g (scant ½ cup) rolled oats

50 g (scant ½ cup) whole wheat flour, plus more for dusting

40 g (¼ cup) sesame seeds (see Top Tip)

25 g (⅛ cup) water

30 g (2 tbsp) olive oil

10 g (1½ tsp) runny honey, or pure maple syrup

3 g (½ tsp) salt, or to taste

Top Tip:
Toast your sesame seeds to really bring out their flavor. Allow them to cool before using them in the dough.

STEP 1: In a mixing bowl, mix together all the ingredients to form a stiff dough in which all of the elements are well incorporated. Cover the bowl with a clean shower cap or your choice of cover, and leave the dough on the counter for 2 to 3 hours, or until you are ready to use it, up to a maximum of 6 hours, if necessary. It will not grow during this time, but the ingredients will have a chance to settle and the flavors will develop.

STEP 2: When you are ready to bake, preheat the oven to 350°F (180°C) convection or 375°F (190°C) conventional. Line a baking sheet with parchment paper.

Dust your counter with a light dusting of flour, turn the dough onto the counter and use a rolling pin to roll out the dough to ⅛ inch (3 mm) thick. Flour the rolling pin to prevent it from sticking and move your dough around as your roll it out, so that it does not stick to the counter. Cut out rounds with a 2½-inch (6-mm) cookie or biscuit cutter. Alternatively, use a pizza cutter or sharp knife to cut the dough into 2½-inch (6-cm) squares. Place the crackers gently on the prepared pan. They can be placed quite close, as the crackers do not spread sideways as they bake. Prick each cracker with a fork to prevent them from puffing up as they bake.

STEP 3: Bake for 7 minutes, remove the pan from the oven, turn the crackers over with a fork and a small metal spatula, return the pan to the oven, then bake for another 7 minutes.

STEP 4: Remove the crackers from the oven and transfer them to a wire rack to cool and crisp up. Serve as soon as they are cooled enough to eat! Store any leftovers in an airtight container.

Einkorn and Hazelnut Oat Crackers

These crackers are made by mixing the dough and leaving it overnight. The flavor will develop and the dough may even puff up slightly, but it is not a necessity. This allows you to mix the dough one day, then leave it on the counter until you want to use it the next day.

I use chopped, roasted hazelnuts in these crackers, which works perfectly with the taste of the einkorn flour. If you do not have hazelnuts, replace them with roasted, finely chopped nuts of your choice.

PREP: Feed all of your starter 60 grams (½ cup) of flour and 60 grams (¼ cup) of water. Allow it to become active and ready to use.

Makes 20 to 24 crackers

100 g (½ cup) active or unfed spare starter

50 g (scant ½ cup) rolled oats

50 g (½ cup) whole grain einkorn flour, plus more for dusting

40 g (¼ cup) finely chopped roasted hazelnuts, or your choice of nut

25 g (⅛ cup) water

30 g (2 tbsp) olive oil

10 g (1½ tsp) runny honey

3 g (½ tsp) salt, or to taste

STEP 1: In a mixing bowl, mix together all the ingredients to form a stiff dough. Ensure that the ingredients are well and evenly combined. Cover the bowl with a clean shower cap or your choice of cover and leave it on the counter overnight.

STEP 2: When ready to bake, preheat the oven to 350°F (180°C) convection or 375°F (190°C) conventional. Line a baking sheet with parchment paper.

Dust your kitchen counter with a little flour, turn the dough out onto the counter and use a rolling pin to roll the dough out to ⅛ inch (3 mm) thick. Flour your rolling pin to prevent it from sticking and move your dough around as you roll it out, so that it does not stick to the counter. Cut out rounds with a 2½-inch (6-mm) cookie or biscuit cutter. Alternatively, use a pizza cutter or sharp knife to cut the dough into 2½-inch (6-cm) squares. Place crackers on the prepared baking pan. They can be placed close as they do not spread sideways as they bake. Prick each cracker with a fork to prevent them from puffing up as they bake.

STEP 3: Bake for 7 minutes on one side, remove the pan from the oven, turn the crackers over with a fork and a small metal spatula, return the pan to the oven, then bake for another 7 minutes.

STEP 4: Remove the crackers from the oven and transfer them to a wire rack to cool slightly. They will crisp up as they cool. Store any leftovers in an airtight container.

Serve as soon as they are cool enough to eat!

How to Make Cooked Grains

These are the methods I use to cook all of my grains to ensure that they are never mushy or bitter for use in bread or in a dish. By using equal volumes of grains and water, and allowing them to fully cook in their own steam, they are always perfectly cooked and wonderfully chewy and separated. Use them immediately for a meal, as an alternative to rice or pasta, or allow them to cool for your dough. Any extra grains can be kept in the fridge for several days, or stored in the freezer in batches until you are ready to use them. Thaw the grains thoroughly before adding to your dough.

It is best to measure these recipes by volume instead of weight. Use a measuring cup, tea cup or mug to measure the grains and the water.

Always allow the grains to cool fully before adding them to any doughs.

Quinoa

1 cup white quinoa

1 cup water

In a small to medium saucepan over medium-high heat, bring the quinoa and water to a boil, then lower the heat to medium-low and allow the quinoa to simmer, uncovered, for 6 minutes.

Turn off the heat, place a lid on the saucepan and leave the grains to continue to cook in the steam for 15 to 20 minutes.

Remove the lid and fork the quinoa to separate it.

Khorasan

¾ cup Khorasan grains

1 cup water

In a small to medium saucepan over medium heat, bring the Khorasan and water to a boil, then lower the heat and allow the grains to simmer, uncovered, for 10 minutes.

Turn off the heat, place a lid on the saucepan and leave the grains to continue to cook in the steam until they have cooled, typically 20 to 25 minutes.

Emmer/Farro/Einkorn/Spelt

1 cup emmer/farro/einkorn/spelt grains

1 cup water

In a small to medium saucepan over medium-high heat, bring the grains and water to a boil, then lower the heat to medium-low and allow the grains to simmer, uncovered, for 6 minutes.

Turn off the heat, place a lid on the saucepan and leave the grains to continue to cook in the steam for 20 to 25 minutes.

Remove the lid and fork the grains to separate them.

How to Roast Seeds and Nuts

To roast seeds or nuts, spread them in a single layer on a large baking sheet and roast at 350°F (180°C) convection or 400°F (200°C) conventional for 15 to 20 minutes, moving the seeds around every 5 minutes to ensure that the seeds around the edges do not overcook. Remove the seeds from the oven and allow them to cool before handling.

Master Recipe Sourdough Baking Timetables

The following is a set of timetables based on my master recipe process (page 27) to show how it can be tailored to fit into your life and environment.

My Typical Master Recipe Timetable

These timings can move slightly either way, typically starting a bit later as the weather warms up, maybe allowing a bit longer when it is colder.

1. At 9:00 a.m., take your starter from the fridge and leave it on the counter with its lid firmly on.

2. At 11:00 a.m., feed your starter, at room temperature, the amount necessary for your baking plans.

3. Cover it again with the lid and leave it to do its work, typically between 3 and 5 hours, depending on the temperature.

4. Start mixing your dough together at around 4:00 p.m.

5. Between 5:00 and 6:00 p.m., perform the first set of pulls and folds.

6. Between then and 9:00 p.m., perform 3 more sets of pulls and folds at whatever random intervals suit your schedule, just when you are passing the bowl; they do not need to be timed.

7. Cover the dough with a clean shower cap or your cover of choice and leave the dough on the counter overnight; this is the process to follow when the overnight temperatures are up to 70°F (20°C).

8. In the morning, typically around 7:00 a.m., or later if it has been a cold night and the dough needs a bit longer, pull the dough together and place it in the banneton, cover it with the same shower cap, and put it into the fridge

9. Bake it directly from the fridge, when you are ready, after a minimum of 3 hours, typically more like 10 hours.

Workday Master Recipe Timetable

The aim of this timetable is to allow you to be able to fit making a full master recipe dough around your working day.

1. Feed your starter directly from the fridge before going to work; by feeding it cold, your starter takes longer to respond, which is perfect on this occasion.

2. Leave the dough somewhere that is not too warm to do its work while you are out. During this time, it may get active, then start to quiet down again, depending on your starter.

3. Once home from work, use the starter directly without feeding it again, to mix the dough together.

4. Over the next 2 hours, perform 3 more sets of pulls and folds. Note: If you get home late or have little time, perform at least 1 full set of pulls and folds on the dough. One set is better than none and will still stimulate the dough. See my Super Lazy Sourdough Master method on page 36 for reference.

(Continued)

5. Cover the dough with a clean shower cap or your cover of choice and leave it on the counter overnight at room temperature, ideally for 8 to 10 hours at 64 to 68°F (18 to 20°C).

6. In the morning, before work, pull the dough into a ball and place it in the banneton, cover it with the same shower cap and place it in the fridge.

7. Bake directly from the fridge when you get home from work.

An Alternative Timetable Based on Feeding the Starter the Night Before

1. Feed your starter and leave it out all night, hopefully at or below 64°F (18°C), covered with a clean shower cap or cover of your choice; it may be a bit deflated by next morning, but hopefully still a bit bubbly.

2. Mix the dough together the next morning when you are ready.

3. After an hour, perform the first set of pulls and folds.

4. Over the next 2 to 3 hours, perform 3 more sets of pulls and folds.

5. Cover the dough with the same shower cap and leave it somewhere not too cold.

6. Before going to bed, pull the dough together. Place it in the banneton, cover it with the same shower cap and place it in the fridge.

7. The next day, bake directly from the fridge when you are ready.

For FAQ and troubleshooting, see page 40.

Acknowledgments

I would like to thank my extended sourdough family. To everyone who follows me on my social media platforms or who has ever liked, commented or messaged me—I am so incredibly grateful for all of your continued support. And to everyone who has ever used my recipes or sent me photos of your foodbod bakes, thank you so much, I love seeing them.

In particular, I would like to thank my amazing Facebook group; the community we have, the sharing, support, creativity and love is overwhelming. I love you guys! Especially, thank you to my amazing support team and my superstar partner.

Special thanks to my superbly talented friends Gill and Jon from Sytch Farm Studios for my beautiful ceramics and wooden pieces, and the lovely Ahren, a.k.a. The Garlic Tun, for my beautiful lames and bread knives.

So much thanks and love to my wonderful friends, my secret recipe testers and tasters and my wonderful support network. You all know who you are, xx.

Massive thanks to everyone at Page Street Publishing for making this happen—you are all amazing, especially Sarah Monroe; this book would not have happened without you. Your foresight, support and guidance have made this a smooth, enjoyable process.

Huge thanks to my photographer, James Kennedy; thank you for sharing my vision and letting my bakes speak for themselves.

Special love to my lovely Caroline and Selma; none of this would be happening without you both. You are both missed daily and never ever forgotten.

My biggest thank you is to my little family: my amazing husband, Graham, my chief taster and beautiful son, Ben, and my constant companion and sourdough fan, Bob the dog.

About the Author

Elaine Boddy has created and run a vegetarian food blog, foodbod, focused on healthy tasty food, for many years. She launched foodbod Sourdough in 2018 to share her sourdough experience and master recipe. She teaches and supports people on the journey of making sourdough daily and teaches sourdough baking in her home kitchen.

Elaine lives in a very small village in the middle of England with her husband, son, and dog, Bob.

Index